The Craigslist Anthologies

SHATTERED

Stories of Violence, Trauma, Addiction,

Strength, and Survival

Created by

Jessica Larkin

This book was made by

Saunders House

ISBN: 979-8-9912537-0-3

Created by: Jessica Larkin
Edited by: Jessica Larkin & Tanita Ross-Cady

Dedication

To my husband, Christopher,

Thank you for saving me, taking my pain away, showing me what real love feels like, and keeping me safe.

Thank you for respecting me, being patient with me in my healing, and loving me at my worst-

You are the calm in my storm

You are my best friend, my lover, and my home today and always.

May we always be somewhere on a beach.

"When you love a girl that has lived trauma, when she realizes that you are choosing to love her, and not hurt her, she will love you back with the same kind of tenacity that it took to walk through fire."

–Tracy Malone

"One's dignity may be assaulted, vandalized, and cruelly mocked, but it can never be taken away unless it is surrendered."

–Michael J. Fox

Trigger Warning

Content Advisory

This anthology contains graphic descriptions and detailed accounts of domestic violence, verbal and physical abuse, stalking, weapons, sexual content, sexually transmitted diseases, miscarriage, profanity, alcohol use, addiction, drug use, and death. The stories within are raw and real, offering unfiltered glimpses into the lives of those who have endured profound trauma and hardship. As such, the material is intended for mature readers over the age of 18.

Purpose of the Warning

Our primary goal is to inform and prepare readers for the intense content they will encounter. We understand that some of the themes explored in this book may be triggering, particularly for those who have had similar experiences. It is crucial to approach this material with awareness and self-care.

Reading Guidelines

Take Breaks: If you find the content overwhelming, give yourself permission to step away and take breaks as needed.

Grounding Techniques: Engage in grounding exercises such as focusing on your breath, feeling the physical sensations of your surroundings, or using a comforting object to help center yourself.

Safe Space: Ensure you are in a safe and comfortable environment while reading. Surround yourself with items that provide a sense of security and calm.

Emotional Check-Ins: Regularly check in with your emotional state. If you begin to feel distressed, pause and allow yourself time to process.

Resources and Support

If you find yourself in need of support, there are resources available to you.

National Domestic Violence Hotline
1-800-799-7233 www.thehotline.org

Substance Abuse and Mental Health Services Administration (SAMHSA) Hotline 1-800-662-HELP (4357)
www.SAMHSA.gov

Crisis Text Line
Text HOME to 741741 for immediate support.
www.crisistextline.org

Compassionate Note

We have crafted this anthology with the utmost care and compassion. It serves as a safe space for women to speak their truths and share their stories. Through understanding the experiences of others, we hope to foster empathy and compassion.

Please approach these narratives with an open heart and know that while the journey through these pages may be challenging, it is also a testament to the resilience of the human spirit.

We hope that by shining a light on these dark experiences, we can contribute to a greater understanding and support for those who endure them.

Table of Contents

Preface

As I write these words, I am filled with a lot of mixed emotions. This experience has been deeply rewarding yet profoundly challenging.

This anthology, comprised by the voices of twenty individuals who have endured domestic violence, sexual abuse, addiction, stalking, trauma, and even death, is not just a collection of stories–

It is a testament of their will to survive.

From the first time my boyfriend laid his hands on me at sixteen, to my harrowing battle for survival in my mid-twenties, I've known despair and the struggle to reclaim my life. But I am not alone in this journey.

This anthology was born out of a need to raise awareness about the silent epidemic plaguing our society, leaving countless individuals isolated in their suffering. Through these narratives, we aim to shatter the silence and offer solace to those who have endured these afflictions.

To the reader, I implore you to heed these stories. They are not dramatic fables, but accounts of raw and brutal human experiences.

Open your eyes to the realities faced by so many and let empathy and understanding guide your future thoughts and actions.

Editing these stories was a challenge filled with both responsibility and privilege. I endeavored to honor the voices of our authors, ensuring their truths rang clear. In the process, I confronted my own demons, reliving past pain.

Amidst the darkness, there is light.

By sharing our experiences, we hope to bridge the gap between ignorance and awareness.

For those who have walked in our shoes, may you find comfort in knowing you are not alone. For those spared by such tribulations, may these stories serve as a wake-up call—to be vigilant, set boundaries, and never underestimate your strength.

Together, let us break the cycle of silence and pave the way for a future where sharing your truth is acceptable, a future free from stigmas and shame.

Introduction

It began over cocktails by the fireplace, in a whirlwind of ideas and aspirations, when a spark of inspiration was ignited. My friend Tanita and I found ourselves immersed in the idea of creating something sincere and impactful. Stories from everyday people like us that could resonate with others and shed light on the shadows of human experience.

Thus, the idea for this anthology series was born—a collection of stories sourced from a platform where we could interact with individuals from all segments of society and get a healthy variation of responses.

I wanted to amplify the voices of those who have endured the darkest of nights, weathered the storms of domestic violence, trauma, sexual abuse, stalking, addiction, and death, yet emerged on the other side with stories to tell and scars to bear.

We turned to Craigslist, casting a wide net in search of individuals willing to share their truths, their pain, and their stories of survival.

The response was overwhelming.

Seventy-two voices echoed through our inboxes, each carrying with them tales of heartbreak and resilience. Among them, twenty women stood out. Their stories were *raw*, unfiltered accounts of pain and suffering, all with an underlying current, a profound sense of courage and determination.

These were the voices we knew needed to be heard, the narratives that deserved a platform.

In the pages that follow, you will encounter the voices of women bearing real and invisible scars—scars etched deep into their souls.

Each story is a testament to the staunch human spirit, a reminder that survival is not just about enduring the pain but finding the strength to carry on...

As I poured over the submissions, including my own accounts of domestic violence and abuse, I was reminded of the power of storytelling—the power to bear witness, to empathize, and to heal. Every story, every voice, weaves together a tapestry of deep suffering, courage, and recovery.

Through these stories, we hope to challenge preconceived notions and stereotypes surrounding abuse.

It's easy to dismiss the pain of others when it remains hidden behind closed doors. But as you delve into the depths of these narratives, you will come to realize that scars are not always visible—they run deep within the fabric of our society, affecting individuals from all walks of life.

Let these stories be a reminder that behind every face, every neighbor, every co-worker, lies a story waiting to be heard. Let us honor the courage and bravery of those who have survived, and pledge to stand together to give support and love to those who have endured violence, addiction, and trauma.

Prologue

In the shadows of silence, behind closed doors and fake smiles, lie the shattered pieces of countless souls.

This anthology is a mosaic of resilience, crafted by the voices of women who have weathered storms of unimaginable pain. Within these pages, you will bear witness to the remarkable narratives of survival and strength. These stories display the haunting specter of abuse in its countless forms and cut deep into the marrow of the human experience.

These women lie bear with their scars and triumphs. Each story, a whisper of pain and a scream of defiance.

Yet, from the depths of despair emerges hope and solidarity, as each woman finds solace in sharing her truth and standing as a testament to the power we have—

The power to take back our lives.

"Shattered" is more than a title; it reflects the permanent mark that trauma leaves on the soul. Like debris scattered in the aftermath of a violent crash, their framework is forever changed, pieces bent, broken, and lost forever.

Their stories etched with an intensity that defies destruction. Their voices demand to be heard, to be acknowledged, and to be a catalyst for change.

As you journey through these pages, prepare to be "Shattered" and remade, to feel the weight of emotions that these women have carried, and to emerge with a newfound awareness and empathy.

Let their stories be a call to action, a plea to end the silence and stigma surrounding abuse, to embrace each other with compassion and understanding, and a catalyst for healing and change in a world too often marred by pain and suffering.

Foreword

By Alexis LaRue

My name is Alexis LaRue, and I am a Child Protective Services/Family Case Manager for the Michigan Department of Health and Human Services.

I grew up middle class, fortunately without any traumatic backstory. My parents were always there for me and my siblings, as well as all my friends who needed a little extra love and to be taken under their wing, Jessica included.

I started my college career a little later than most. After completing my Criminal Justice degree in 2015, I found a job where I could work with children and make a real difference in their lives. I wanted to help put an end to the struggles they endured; it was my dream to help find them a path to healing and growth into adulthood.

I am passionate about the topics in this anthology, as I work closely with individuals who have endured the pain and suffering that each author has had the courage to share within these pages. It is an honor and a privilege to discuss my lifelong friendship with the creator of "Shattered" and to acknowledge the impactful anthology that I have just digested.

As teenagers, Jessica and I were thick as thieves, always out running the streets and getting into trouble with our friends. Staying out past curfew and the occasional Minor in possession of alcohol, just good ole teenage troublemakers. Our friendship has weathered many storms, and many tough relationships, hers often characterized by domestic violence…

The impact of substance abuse and legal issues is life altering, and the loss of many friends along the way to drugs and alcohol has been heartbreaking.

Despite these hardships, we've grown and celebrated each other's victories along the way, maturing together into adulthood. Through it all, Jessica has consistently exceeded my expectations. "The Craigslist Anthologies: Shattered" stands as another major accomplishment in her journey through life.

My time in Children's Protective Services has been emotional, exhausting, stressful, happy, sad, and just about every other emotion you can think of. I work closely with families, regularly managing a large caseload of adults and children who have seen the horrors that happen behind closed doors. Unspeakable tragedies and heartbreaking outcomes are a huge part of my daily life.

I have seen firsthand the situations that the women in this anthology have been through, and I see people hit rock bottom more often than I would like to admit. You do your best as a Case Manager to support them and give them the right tools, but ultimately where they go from there is up to them.

Human experience is such a personal, intimate, and impactful process that continues to shape us until the day we die. Even though we have remained incredibly close over the years, Jessica had only shared bits and pieces of the hell she went through after her move to California.

After reading the intimate details of this book and the full story of what she went through, I found deep empathy washing over me, not just for her but for each one of the authors.

The voices in this anthology roar loud, sharing experiences that are not often discussed and feelings that are usually kept silent. This collection of stories provides a broader and more comprehensive view of these issues than you would get from just one person's narrative. I felt compelled to keep turning the pages to hear all the voices ready to share their truth.

Shattered will have a different takeaway for every single person who reads it. For some, it will be relatable and comforting—to know that in their darkest hours, others were going through similar experiences. It could be retraumatizing for those who have lived through abuse and trauma. These stories may trigger painful memories and emotions.

Proceed with caution and honor your own well-being. Practice self-care, embrace breathing techniques, and ground yourself in the present moment if the weight of these narratives becomes too heavy to bear. Trauma and how it's treated can positively or negatively impact every part of your life if you allow it to. It can destroy confidence built over years with one bad relationship and one narcissistic person.

Untreated trauma can turn the most amazing men into heavy-handed husbands once triggered. It can take an innocent little girl, once defiled, and lead her down a path of destruction and abuse that most people couldn't imagine.

This anthology is important because it connects people, no matter their individual situation. You never really know the battle being fought behind others' doors.

There is a strong message and call to empathy and understanding that sets "Shattered" apart from other publications on trauma, addiction, and survival.

In my career in Children's Protective Services, I have always felt this way, and even more so now: I encourage everyone reading this to be kind to one another. As you read through these personal experiences, remember that the unbearable co-worker may be a battered woman behind closed doors.

The rude parking lot attendant may be on their twentieth day sober, fighting every hour just to survive the next, each minute seeming agonizing. The new girlfriend who seems self-conscious about her body, even though she's gorgeous, may have been abused for years at the hands of her father.

For those who have lived, loved, survived, overcame, and continue doing so every day, I invite you to traverse these treacherous terrains alongside me.

Here, there's no room for sugar-coating or glossing over the harsh realities we've endured.

Instead, every word bears the weight of truth, every narrative a testament to the lasting imprint that suffering leaves upon the soul. It is a testament to the resilience of the human spirit and the power of sharing our stories to foster empathy, understanding, and ultimately, change.

Dive into these pages with an open mind and heart and let the voices within guide you toward a deeper awareness of the hidden struggles happening all around us.

May this anthology be a source of hope for those still lost in the darkness. There is indeed life after abuse—a life filled with love, joy, respect, and above all, safety. With empathy as our guide, let us embark on this journey together, forging a path toward a future where no one suffers in silence.

Ragdoll

by Allison Halphren

My name is Ally, and I'm 35 years old.

I stand as a survivor of severe domestic violence; enduring mental, physical, and sexual abuse. Throughout my journey, my goal has been to illuminate the truth for those who remain uninformed about such harrowing experiences, lacking the empathy necessary for understanding.

At the same time, I aspire to instill hope in girls who, like me, find themselves entangled in similar circumstances, offering them the promise of a way out, even when faced with the darkest of times.

I won't deny it; before I found myself in the grip of the most traumatic abuse I've ever experienced, I too, shared the common misconception of many.

I would naively advise friends to simply leave their situations or call the police, thinking it was just that straightforward. I now recognize the depth of my obliviousness and am profoundly sorry for it.

It took becoming a victim myself to truly understand the complexities of abuse. Never in my wildest dreams did I imagine I would find myself in such a situation.

I find gratitude in the newfound understanding I have gained regarding the depth and severity of abuse. This mindfulness has ignited within me a passionate drive to raise awareness and support those around me who are currently struggling with similar situations.

Like countless others, my story begins with meeting someone who initially made me feel safe, valued, and loved. At first, he seemed like the epitome of perfection – a common narrative. Yet, that illusion quickly shattered. I found myself gradually entangled in a web of manipulation, to the point where I felt as though my mind had been taken over…

My choices and actions were no longer my own. It wasn't until later, with a chilling realization, that I understood the depth of my entrapment. It was akin to being held hostage, trapped in a situation from which escape seemed damn near impossible.

The memory of the first time he hit me is etched in my mind like a scar on my soul.

It happened very early on in our relationship, during a seemingly harmless evening at his friend's house.

The couple who owned the place had retreated to their room, leaving us alone in the guest bedroom for the evening.

Wanting to surprise him, I slipped into a seductive outfit, anticipating his return from a quick shower. The bedroom door, however, refused to close entirely, leaving a small gap - a detail I never imagined would become so significant.

When he reappeared, instead of pleasure, I was met with a sudden eruption of rage.

He hurled insults at me, stripping away any sense of dignity I had, reducing me to nothing more than a "whore." In a blur of violence, he shoved me into the closet and unleashed a barrage of blows upon me, each strike leaving its mark - half my teeth knocked out, a dent in my forehead, a blackened eye, painful knots littering my skull.

It was a moment that forever altered the trajectory of my life, marking the beginning of a nightmare I couldn't wake up from.

That initial instance of abuse left me engulfed in a whirlwind of emotions, shame, confusion, and seething anger. When the opportunity to escape finally presented itself, I seized it with all the strength I could muster. I ran, because my life depended on it, each stride fueled by a fierce determination and a promise to myself: I would never allow him back into my life.

'How could he betray the trust I had placed in him?' The very foundation of our relationship had been destroyed.

The following day, a twist of fate intervened when he was arrested for a probation violation, abruptly disappearing from my life for two long months.

During that time, I gradually began to heal, pushing him out of my mind as I focused on moving forward. Yet, just when I thought I had left the nightmare behind, he resurfaced.

His apology seemed sincere, his words laced with promises of change and redemption. He attributed his actions to past hurts and insecurities, vowing that he would never repeat his abusive behavior.

In a moment of vulnerability and perhaps naivety, I allowed myself to believe him, clinging to the hope that this time would be different.

As time wore on, the insidious grip of manipulation tightened around me, and I became unknowingly under his complete control.

My sense of self was systematically eroded until I believed that my sole purpose was to please him.

He wielded power over every aspect of my life, starting with confiscating my phone, and forcing me to sever ties with friends and family, leaving me isolated and vulnerable. His control extended to even the most mundane decisions, dictating what clothes I put on in the morning, how I wore my makeup, and enforcing strict rules, forbidding any interaction with his friends.

I was not even allowed to utter a simple Hello.

The consequences of disobedience were swift and brutal.

It was a vicious cycle of punishment inflicted with relentless force, always targeting my face or head, a constant reminder of my subservience.

Eventually, fear became my constant companion, dictating every move I made. I walked with my eyes glued to the sidewalk, afraid to lift them even for a fleeting glimpse of my surroundings or a passing storefront. Any momentary lapse, any inadvertent glance in the direction of another person, regardless of age or appearance, would trigger his irrational jealousy.

He would seize the slightest opportunity to accuse me of lewd intentions, conjuring unfounded accusations of wanting to engage in illicit activities with strangers. And inevitably, these baseless suspicions culminated in the same grim routine...

A storm of ruthless blows raining down upon me, leaving me battered and bruised, if I was fortunate enough to escape with only that.

The horror of my ordeal escalated to a point where he attempted to snuff out my very existence. His warped insecurity drove him to punish me, all in a twisted effort to disfigure and "ugly" me, as he callously put it.

He believed that by rendering me physically repulsive, he could ensure that no one else would ever want me. In addition to enduring physical assaults daily, I was subjected to excruciating, degrading acts of sexual violence.

He would demand hours of forceful, agonizing intercourse, deriving sick pleasure from my pain and suffering. I was forced to utter repulsive phrases, begging for the very violation he was inflicting upon me, under the threat of even more violent punishments if I dared to resist.

22

My life was a nightmare within a nightmare, a grotesque reality where the sanctity of consent was mercilessly violated, and the lines between love and cruelty blurred beyond recognition.

Despite my desperate attempts to comply, to appease his insatiable appetite for control, I realized with chilling clarity that no amount of perfection could shield me from his unrelenting cruelty.

His violence knew no bounds; he would seize any perceived infraction or fabricate an excuse to unleash his fury upon me. Once his rage had been satiated with blows to my head, leaving me dazed and battered, he would imprison me within the confines of our apartment. Leaving me in hell, alone, and bleeding, as he disappeared into the night.

The inventory of humiliations and betrayals I endured at his hands is too vast to summarize in these pages. From his constant deceitful schemes designed to inflict continuous pain, to recklessly chasing me down the street, where I narrowly escaped being struck by passing cars.

Amidst the endless nightmare I endured, there were two occasions that stand out to me, moments when I truly believed he intended to kill me.

It's crucial to interject with a vital detail: This man was deeply rooted in gang culture.

From the tender age of 14, he had been involved in violent confrontations, honing his skills as a fighter. His hands, I can only describe as remarkable weapons, were akin to those of a professional UFC fighter. With a physique resembling that of a football player, towering at a staggering 250 pounds, his sheer size was overwhelming compared to my petite frame of 120 pounds.

His blows were not merely forceful; they were brutal, bordering on lethal. Each strike, a devastating assault, leaving me defenseless against his overwhelming strength and ferocity.

The first of these harrowing encounters occurred over a seemingly trivial incident: a shirt accidentally slipped off a chair and into a puddle of water that had pooled from our leaking water heater. His reaction was swift and savage, unleashing his rage upon me - eight consecutive blows to my face and head with such force that I felt as though each punch was shattering my skull.

Then, he threw me to the ground and viciously yanked me up by my hair, slamming my skull once again, against the concrete floor.

The repercussions of that brutal assault would haunt me for years to come, as I now live with the devastating effects of a chronic brain injury, a permanent reminder of the violence I endured.

In the aftermath of this vicious attack, my battered and swollen face bore little resemblance to my former self, a grotesque testament to the savagery of his actions.

Seeking refuge and assistance, I fled to a clinic in desperate need of help, hoping that someone would intervene and offer sanctuary. However, my cries for help fell on deaf ears, as I was met with indifference and apathy. Despite my shattered spirit and mangled appearance, my abuser's grip on me remained immovable.

Within the span of a mere hour, he hunted me down and issued a chilling ultimatum:

Leave, and I will kill you.

The second terrifying episode unfolded during a seemingly routine outing on our bikes, a simple excursion that spiraled into chaos over a casual comment I made. In a fit of rage, he callously kicked me off my bike, leaving me abandoned as he took my bike and sped away into the distance.

It was yet another instance of his explosive temper, his volatility escalating with each passing day.

Amidst the cycle of abuse, I began to notice a pattern: brutality intensified to a crescendo once a week.

Terrified and with no safe haven in sight, I would flee, seeking refuge on the nightly bus route from Huntington Park to LAX. Night after night, I traversed the cityscape, clinging to the fleeting moments of relief offered by the hum of the bus, a small moment of peace was all it offered me, before I was thrust back into my dark reality.

Yet, on this particular night, something within me shifted. Faced with the prospect of returning home, heading straight into unavoidable danger. I grappled with the agonizing decision before me. Desperate for any sign of his whereabouts, I resorted to relentless calls to his phone, met only with the beep of his voicemail. In a moment of desperation and defiance, I veered off the beaten path, venturing down an alleyway that held the promise of his whereabouts, disregarding the ominous risk I was taking.

As I arrived at the gathering in the alley, I found solace in the presence of familiar faces, including his friend's girlfriend.

In my vulnerable state, her presence offered a glimmer of reassurance, a small hope that I wouldn't face this ordeal alone.

With tears staining my cheeks, I pleaded with her to lend me her phone, grasping at the slender thread of possibility that he would answer, giving me some delusional semblance of comfort or security.

He was furious with me, his voice dripping with thinly veiled menace. Despite his hollow assurances that he wouldn't harm me, the underlying threat lingered in the air, it was a constant palpable reminder of the danger that awaited my return.

Fueled by a cocktail of fear and submission, I hurried back, clinging to the fragile hope that this time would be different, that he would keep his promise and spare me from further torment.

The moment I stepped through the door, I was slammed against the wall with a force that knocked the breath from my lungs. His hands closed around my throat, squeezing with a vice-like grip until the world began to blur and fade. As I teetered on the brink of consciousness, he released his hold, but this was far from over. His accusations rang out like thunder, each word laced with venom and unfounded rage.

He exploded about my supposed transgressions, fueled by baseless rumors, and twisted jealousy.

In his manic fury, he grabbed a screwdriver, wielded with lethal intent. Terror gripped me as he hunted me, the sharp point of the tool raised to strike.

Shock and horror washed over me as I stared down at the metallic protrusion, disbelief coursing through my veins. A six-inch screwdriver was embedded deep within my knee.

Even as I writhed in agony, he continued his assault, his giant hands ceaselessly hitting me, over and over and over. Finally, he forced me into submission, binding me to a chair.

From that moment on, my every word was dictated by his iron will, leaving me, but a hostage in my own home, stripped of my freedom, left to bleed out, on the kitchen floor.

After enduring an agonizing five hours in his oppressive presence, my knee throbbed with unbearable pain, rendering me unable to walk.

Reluctantly, he acknowledged the severity of my injury, admitting that immediate medical attention was needed.

Despite the risk of exposure, he made the surprising decision to send me to the emergency room, all under the mask of concern. I knew it was a lie, but I would take any excuse he would give me to escape.

Calling an Uber, he sent me to the hospital, placing a fragile trust in my silence. As I underwent surgery to remove the embedded screwdriver from my knee, the gravity of my situation became painfully clear. I realized how dangerously close I had come to death, the screwdriver's proximity to a vital artery serving as a chilling reminder of the mortal danger I had faced.

In hindsight, I count myself fortunate to have survived such a horrific ordeal. Yet, even as I rested in the hospital, his threats loomed large in my mind, a haunting reminder of the fragile grip on life I had maintained in the clutches of my tormentor.

Despite my attempts to deflect suspicion by fabricating a tale of a random attack, this wasn't the doctors first rodeo, and they saw through the facade.

As they conducted a thorough examination of my battered body, the truth could not be denied.

The telltale signs of domestic violence were written in bold, the bruises and scars, too numerous to ignore.

Though they maintained a facade of neutrality, their quiet acknowledgment spoke volumes. Their support offered a silent reassurance that I was not alone in my struggle.

Eventually, a compassionate social worker entered the room, her gentle demeanor a stark contrast to the brutality I was used to. With quiet persistence, she urged me to consider seeking refuge in a shelter for abused women, offering a lifeline to escape the cycle of violence that had ensnared me.

Though the path ahead was fraught with uncertainty, her words planted a seed of courage, igniting a fire inside my soul, the thought of a future free from fear and pain was in fact, attainable.

Despite the offers for assistance, I stubbornly clung to the belief that I could navigate this on my own, convinced that I was somehow above seeking refuge in a shelter. Tragically, this misguided determination only prolonged my suffering, allowing the violence to persist for another agonizing six months.

One fateful morning, a team of police officers arrived at our home, their presence a sign of long-awaited justice. With swift precision, they apprehended him on an outstanding warrant, ushering him back behind bars for another 180 days.

Left alone in our apartment with only our cats for company, I found myself grappling with the aftermath of his arrest. The tumultuous events surrounding his incarceration had not gone unnoticed, and soon, the repercussions began to unfold. The owner of our apartment, informed of the chaos, swiftly moved to evict me from the premises, severing the final ties to the hellish existence I had endured for far too long.

In the wake of his arrest and my subsequent eviction, a newfound sense of liberation washed over me.

Though the scars of his abuse would linger, I found comfort in the knowledge that I was finally free from his tyranny, poised to embark on a journey toward healing and redemption.

In the depths of my desperation, I reached out to a trusted friend, laying bare my vulnerability and pleading for sanctuary. Without hesitation, she opened her home to me, providing a temporary refuge from the storm that had ravaged my life.

Yet fate had another surprise in store for me.

A chance encounter led me to a kind-hearted individual who offered me not just shelter, but genuine compassion and support.

Despite my lingering doubts and fears, I accepted his generous offer, allowing myself to believe, however tentatively, that perhaps this time, things could be different.

As I settled into my newfound place of peace, a sense of cautious optimism began to take root within me. For the first time in what felt like an eternity, I dared to entertain the possibility of a future free of pain and fear.

Looking back, I can't help but acknowledge the foolishness of my past decisions, the blind faith I placed in a man who sought to harm me. Yet, even in the face of my own shortcomings, I am grateful for the moments that guided me toward this path of healing and salvation.

The pull of the familiar, the allure of street life, proved to be a powerful force, leading me down a path of self-destruction and despair.

In my moments of weakness, I found myself drawn back into his toxic orbit, seeking solace in the very arms that had brought me so much pain.

Yet, with each passing day, the veil of delusion began to lift, and I found myself confronting the reality of my situation.

The mental abuse I endured served as an assault on my spirit, chipping away at my self-worth until I had nothing left, and I could no longer deny the truth—

I deserved better.

The turning point came in a moment of stark clarity, an awakening that finally destroyed the illusion of love I had clung to for so long. A callous act of violence, inflicted in front of his friends without a shred of remorse. I was humiliated and shocked, he was showing his true colors in public, not behind the safety of closed doors.

This served as a harsh reminder, confirming the depths of his cruelty, he had no shame, he wore his demons on his sleeve.

In that moment, something inside me snapped.

With a newfound resolve, I made a split-second decision to reclaim my freedom, to break free from the chains that bound me to him.

With adrenaline coursing through my veins, I fled with a single-minded determination, leaving behind the wreckage of my past and never looking back.

As I boarded the bus and journeyed far away from the darkness that had consumed me, I felt a sense of liberation wash over me. Though the road ahead was uncertain, I knew with unwavering confidence that I had taken the first step toward reclaiming my life, my dignity, and my soul. I stared out the window and smiled, a feeling rushing through my body that I had not felt in longer than I care to admit.

Then one day fate intervened, delivering a semblance of justice in the form of his incarceration. Knowing that he would be behind bars for the next five years brought a sense of relief and closure that I hadn't dared to hope for.

Finally, I was totally free of his tyranny, free to rebuild my life on my own terms, free to have a future where no one else would be able to dictate my life.

Shortly after his arrest my rescuer arrived, the man who would become my salvation.

Though he may not ever fully grasp the extent of the horrors I endured, his unwavering support and love have been a lifeline in my darkest moments. I understand that it's difficult for him to comprehend the depths of my suffering, having never walked in my shoes.

Yet, despite the lingering scars of my past, I am grateful for his presence in my life, for the warmth of his embrace and the steadiness of his love.

As we embark on this journey together, I am filled with a profound sense of gratitude and hope.

Though the road ahead may be filled with challenges, I know that if we face them together, we can weather any storm.

As I reflect on the trials and tribulations that brought me to this moment, I am reminded of the resilience of the human spirit, the capacity for healing, and renewal in the face of unimaginable adversity.

The scars of my past continue to affect me deeply, manifesting in the form of fear, PTSD, and social withdrawal.

Healing from such profound trauma is a journey, one that requires patience, self-compassion, and support.

It takes immense strength to confront the broken pieces that you are left with after living with abuse and even more to speak out about your experiences.

I urge you to share your stories and be a voice for those without one. Though it has deeply affected my life, I refuse to be silenced and am committed to using my voice to expose the reality of domestic violence.

By sharing your story, you not only honor your own strength but also offer hope and inspiration to others who may be trapped in similar situations. Your courage serves as a reminder that healing is possible, and that no one should ever have to suffer in silence.

As you continue to navigate this path, know that you are not alone. There are countless others who have walked a similar road, who understand the complexities of your experience and stand ready to offer their commonality and empathy.

As you continue your journey of healing and self-discovery, may you find strength in your own resilience, solace in the support of others, and a renewed sense of purpose in sharing your story with the world. Your voice is a powerful force for change, and your story has the potential to spark conversations, raise awareness, and ultimately, inspire healing and transformation.

By sharing your journey, you inspire others to believe in their own strength and worthiness.

Your willingness to extend a hand of support to those in need, by simply offering a listening ear, a shoulder to lean on, and a source of guidance, you provide a lifeline to those who may feel isolated and powerless.

Your words carry the power to uplift and empower, offering a message of hope and encouragement to anyone who may be struggling. Remind them that they are deserving of love, respect, and safety, and that they have the right to reclaim their dignity and independence.

May your messages resonate far and wide, reaching those who need it most and reminding them that they are worthy of a life free from fear and violence.

Your courage in speaking out and offering support is the foundation in the fight against abuse, and your willingness to stand up for others is a testament to your strength and resilience.

This has become an epidemic and I am desperate to give courage to those who have lost hope.

If you are in an abusive situation, just know that there is light at the end of the tunnel–

If you want it.

There is more to life than being someone's ragdoll. Every single woman is beautiful, and you have more self-worth than you can imagine.

You will get through this; you are not alone.

Breaking Point

by Margaret Belvedere

It was below freezing
The sun was starting to come up
My head was pounding

Jesus it's bright out here

I had just crawled out of some basement afterparty
Still in my "not so sexy anymore" bar outfit

Where did I get this sweatshirt?
My mouth tastes disgusting
Please let there be a bottle of water in here

My car was the only one in
the Waterworks Car Wash parking lot
How fitting

I ashed my cigarette
Digging for change in every inch of my vehicle

Fuck I'm a mess
Why aren't my gloves in my purse?

I found earmuffs under all the scattered belongings in my
backseat

I lit another cigarette off my last

His blood was everywhere
The pumping heat was starting to make it smell

My boots crunched through the snow
as I crossed the parking lot

Clink, clink, clink
Clink, clink, clink

FUCK

I put my head between my knees as I squatted
to pick up the untaken change

I tucked my hands in my jacket sleeves
to warm them for a few seconds

One hard sniff and the cocaine remanence
hit the back of my throat–
Fuel to get this done and get home

Clink, clink, clink
Clink, clink, clink

The cleaning wipes dispensed from the machine

As I scrubbed the splatter--
Flashes from the night before resurfaced

Coming out of the alcohol fueled fog
The cars exhaust rushing in front of my headlights
The dinging of the open car door
The bitter-cold air
ripping at my throat as I screamed

The ice scraping my back
as he pulled me across the parking lot

The clumps of my hair in the snow
The salt of my tears
The rage in his eyes

Why did we get back in the car?
He wasn't coming with me
Ohhh, I called Justin to pick him up

It was all coming back to me
I pulled into some random dental office parking lot

I bet that's where my gloves are
Jesus why did I go to that after party?
Everyone probably thinks I'm an idiot
Just showing up covered in blood like a psycho

I'm so embarrassed
I need more wipes

Clink, clink, clink
Clink, clink, clink

He grabbed my hair again and pulled hard
This time I swung harder
His nose exploded

I scrubbed viciously

When was this going to end?
Why can't we stop fighting like this?

Tears aided in my cleaning efforts

I love him so much
I don't know how to let him go

My passenger floorboard looked like the
aftermath of a medical response team

I took a beat
The sun felt warm on my cheek
I lit another cigarette
I closed my eyes

I need to let him go
The only way to do that is to get away
I have to leave this place

I took a long hard drag
Tears streamed down my cheeks

It was 7am
I hadn't felt my bed sheets in over 24 hours

I can't live like this anymore

I walked the crime scene evidence to the trash

A cloud of smoke cleared in front of me
as I turned to head back to my car

Reality was suddenly there

There I was at a ghetto ass park and wash
Cleaning his blood off my dash at dawn

I don't know how I got this deep
The only way to get out of this is to disappear

I started my engine
Put my sunglasses on
One more hard sniff

Now all I needed was a plan

The Little Voice
by Lisa Postert

He was tall
Light brown skin and tattooed
He was just my type

I was Intoxicated
I felt so special
I was high on his pedestal
He was sixteen years younger than me

What did I do to deserve this kind of attention?

We were crazy about each other
from the moment we met
Inseparable

I was head over heels in love
with the master manipulator

That's what his friends called him
He had the gift of gab

That was the first time
the little voice inside my head spoke to me
She told me to run
This was my deepest regret–
That I rejected the warning

I willingly walked straight into the darkness

My little voice knew what was coming
I was too distracted to see it

He had a tough life
He deserved to be loved
I tended to those wounds
I selflessly gave him all my energy

I took him in when he was homeless
I supported him
I gave him an ear to listen
I gave him a shoulder to cry on

He had been through hell—
Now I was living there with him

We were both not working
We were not following our dreams and ambitions
We were doing drugs

He started getting paranoid
He started to accuse me of cheating

Looking back now it was so clear—
He was projecting his actions on me

In the end he was the cheater

My nights were endless arguments
My days were spent trying to make it up to him
The drugs were doing what they do–
Destroying us

My little voice was getting louder
But still I neglected her

I was so in love with him I couldn't see straight
He couldn't see straight because he was high
His hateful words turned into bruises
My loving support turned to shame
I was crumbling inside

My reflection was unrecognizable
I had never been through this kind of abuse

I didn't know what was happening until it was too late
I was desperately trying to fix him
I was in too deep
At this point I couldn't even fix myself

My little voice was sounding the alarm
'GET THE FUCK OUT'

But I stayed

She was the only one who could see it coming–
My little voice

I finally knew the truth
I had proof he cheated
I just needed one more drink
to find the courage to confront him

The lies
The deceit
My insides were imploding
My tongue was sharp
His left hook sharper

This time it hit harder
This time he broke my jaw
He got six years in prison

I got my jaw wired shut
A liquid diet and a metal plate

My little voice said
I told you so

Neon Lights

by Carly Graves

A sea of bodies
    Intense pulsing lights
        I am just a silhouette in a sweaty crowd

Blending in with the others
Hiding from my reality

The weight of motherhood
Constantly tugging at the seams
        The seams of my soul
      The seams of my scantily clad dreams

My parents at home with my child
My precious boy—

My soul profoundly voided and annoyed
      My laughter and smile
        An ever-shining veneer
      The pressure they put on me to be perfect

It is unbearable

I can never do anything right
A perpetual fuck up
What will it take to make them proud
I will never be enough

One more drink to ease my pain
    One step closer
        to drowning out my uncomfortable reality

The clock is ticking
I must face motherhood soon

I hate it—I hate myself
I hate that I must lie to be here
    That this is supposed to be fun
        I hate that I always have to pretend

Why isn't home with him better than this?
Why do I choose this dance floor?

I hate watching all of the other girls be happy
Alive and unfazed
No reality
No responsibility

No curfew
No alarm
No baby screaming at sunrise

Just Free

I am always pretending
        Consumed by guilt
            I don't want this life
            I don't want this responsibility

Freedom

Something I can always see
But never touch

I will never feel that lightness again
because now I'm a mom

My dreams unreachable
        A relentless grind
            Trapped by my decisions
                Too late to be undone
My child a tether

A life I wish I could rewrite
        Is that why I'm always out chasing shadows
            In the neon light?

Yet every chance I get
        I put on my sequined guise
            Always seeking connection
                in the wrong places

Looking for love in a stranger's eyes

I Just dance through the heartache
I dance to keep sane
The rhythm and chaos
somehow eases my pain

Dreaming of the day I can truly be free

A present mother, just my son and me.

The Mask
by Margaret Belvedere

I was desperate
alone

Four months ago, I had moved across the country
I was trying to start a new life
I had just graduated college–
With honors
Twice

I was a Registered Diagnostic Cardiac Sonographer with a BA

A 700-credit score

I had a brand-new car and
a two-bedroom apartment
in Orange County California

I was 25
I was beautiful, ambitious, outgoing
My laughter was contagious

The possibilities were endless–
but I was
broke

Broke was an understatement
Never had I experienced this level of poverty
I was struggling hard

I couldn't find a big girl job
I had willingly demoted myself to a waitress

The time clock started at 10am and
didn't end until 2am
seven days a week

I would have done just about anything to
get ahead of this financial situation

The end felt non-existent

With the little time I had
I was trying to meet people

I was single and ready to mingle
What was the harm in a friendly introduction?
Little did I know I was the perfect target

The cigarette smoke cleared
as he walked into the bar

He was tall, his green eyes
like magnets to mine
His voice was so deep that it pulled me toward him
like a Josh Turner Song

We were born and raised in the same state
He was a US Marine

I had stars in my eyes

He paid our tab and grabbed my hand
We left together

But I had no idea—

That he was leading me

straight into hell

Obsession

by Tanya Joy Sprague

I punched the time clock.
My heart was racing, and my palms were sweating.
My insides were all twisted up.

I knew he was watching me.

I had my manager escort me to the car.
My doors locked and the keys were in the ignition–
I had to get out of here before he saw me.

Thank God my roommate was home.
I didn't want to be alone.

Buzz buzz buzz
Buzz buzz buzz
Buzz buzz buzz

He wouldn't stop calling.
I threw my phone in my purse.
Tears welled in my eyes, I just needed to get home.

I was tucked in safe in my roommate's bed.
The lights were off, and the doors were all locked.
My mind raced; I wasn't safe anymore.

The next morning, I crept into my room–

Do I dare open the blinds?

It's light out now. I don't need to be afraid.

When I pulled the string, my heart dropped.
Goosebumps covered my body.
His beer cans were in the grass outside my window.

He was here last night.
He was watching.

When I met David, we were coworkers.
After I left that job, he asked me out on a date.
We went for drinks and hit it off quickly.
He was older and so nice to me–

He was a real man's man.
The sex was amazing.
I loved being around him.

Within a few weeks he demanded exclusivity.
I said yes because I wanted to make him happy.
I should have listened to my gut.

I should have run.

He pushed my boundaries.
He pushed my friends and family out of my life.
He pushed my fucking buttons.
He wanted me at his beckoning call 24/7.
He would do really shitty things then follow it up with flowers
and convincing apologies– I would forgive him
I would accept this behavior.

He told me that:
"I worked too much."
"I didn't pay for enough."
"I spent too much time with my friends."

He blamed me.
He shamed me.
He berated me.
He controlled me.

After our last fight he peeled out of the parking lot–

What am I doing?
This is going to shit fast…
Is it worth it?

For three hours my phone rang.
I did NOT want to talk to him.
The next day he was at my front door with flowers
but I sent him away–

Flowers didn't fix anything.
We had real problems.

By then it was Thanksgiving and we had only been dating six
weeks. He was mad that I wanted to spend the day with my
family.
He begged me to see him later, so I agreed to meet him for a
drink. I knew when I left the house that this was a bad idea–

He chose a hotel in Little Italy.

I made sure my family knew what room we were in.
I realized then that I was actually scared for my safety.

I arrived at the hotel, shaking.
He was clearly agitated.

We went to the room so he could change.
His belt didn't fit then it went flying across the room—
Next were his shoes.
Next it was going to be me.

I had to get out of there.

We went down to get a table; his blood was boiling.

Everything was taking too long…

With wine in hand, I tried to salvage what was left of the
       ng. I counted the minutes until I could leave.
              d across the table and grabbed my wrist then yanked

              my bracelet?"

utter

H YOUR OUTFIT. YOU

I MADE IT FOR YOU."

That was the last straw, tomorrow I was leaving him.

The next twenty-four days of my life were a living hell.
I was being followed, watched, and stalked.
My phone rang off the hook.

He showed up at my house.
He showed up at my work.
He called pretending to be someone else to try and get my work schedule.
He stalked me on social media.

I had nowhere to hide.

I couldn't take it anymore, so I went down to the courthouse. I was forced to relive the nightmare that had been my life for the last two months. The judge granted me a *temporary* Domestic Violence restraining order.

Six months of safety…
That's what the little piece of paper promised.

The day before the six months was up, he started using h' friends as weapons. He desperately tried to get to me w sending me pornography and salacious messages.

I started to unravel.
The tears seemed endless.
Fear plagued my mind.

I was constantly looking over my shoulder.

The fun-loving confident woman I was nine weeks ago was gone. She was replaced with someone I had never seen.

I was timid and terrified—
She was a person I didn't recognize anymore.

I went to the courthouse the next day.
I was going to take back my life.

The judge granted me a three-year DVRO.
I wasn't sure if I was entirely free

but for the first time in a little over two months

I could breathe again.

The Glue
by Quinn Wilde

She stands alone in her struggle
A silent scream *echoes*
through the corridors of her soul
In the depths of her despair

The demon's claw *at her spirit*

Her marriage a barren landscape
No friends to share her burdens
Nothing to ignite her passion

Where love once bloomed now all is

but withered

Her job a prison of unfulfilled dreams
The weight too heavy for her weary shoulders
Each day a monotonous march
through a labyrinth of discontent

She yearns deeply for a new beginning
A chance to rewrite her narrative

Searching in the darkness looking for the light
Any small glimmer of hope amidst the shadows

She is a fighter reclaiming her authority.

With each step forward she redefines the odds

In her silence she finds strength
She believes in the resilience born from hardship

It's the only path she has ever known

She will break free from the chains that bind her soul
She will walk with courage in her heart
She knows that what is within her holds the power

The journey will not be easy—

She will not just glue together
the broken pieces that remain

She will create something new from the wreckage
She will emerge from the ashes

This time her scream will be heard
This time she will face the demons

This time—

It is her turn

Intoxicated
by Margaret Belvedere

We were in love
I finally had a partner

I wasn't alone
I was finally experiencing living in my new life

Friends, dinners, gifts, cash, trips, Vegas
It was a whole new world

I felt alive again

No one had ever stroked my love language
quite the way he did

I inhaled him
I was in the clouds
I couldn't see

I hadn't even scratched the surface
I had no idea what was coming

It was too late before I even realized
how deep I was
already

Very quickly–
He became chaotic

Exhausting
No lack of problems

Constant drama

I was playing capture the red flag–

But I loved him

Didn't he deserve love too?
Even if he was broken?

I could handle it
I could handle him

I was strong enough
I had been through this before
I was a badass Bitch from Detroit

I could handle a wounded Marine

Couldn't I?

Goodbye Letter
by Riley Sterling

Dear Alcohol,

I told you last week that I needed some space, and we haven't spoken since. I just thought I should reach out and let you know how I am feeling.

The last eight days have been hard without you, but it has also offered me some clarity and reflection in our relationship. We have been together for the last twenty-three years, and for the most part we have spent time together every day.

My most cherished memories happened in our years together.

They were some of the best times of my life, but in that time, you have also brought me shame, embarrassment, and regret.

I have decided that we need to continue to take time away from each other. I have needed to set some boundaries for a long time; I need my own life, and right now—

That is a life without you in it.

Recently I have felt more than ever that you have taken over my life and I have no control. I need that to change and that is why I am taking a step back.

I need to find myself, a new me, a me that is not attached to you. I will decide when we meet and how much time we spend together.

You are no longer in control.

I will be making these decisions moving forward.

Just because I love you and you are my friend does not mean we have to see each other every day. Please don't be sad, you will still be with me on holidays, birthdays, vacations, and special occasions. I promise you won't miss out. However, making you my priority daily can no longer continue.

Alcohol, you have been there for me to celebrate so many BIG moments in my life. New jobs, graduations, making big career moves, meeting new friends, visiting old friends, celebrations, vacations, and some of the best memories, memories I will treasure forever.

You were there to help protect me through some of my hardest times.

The ache of a heartbreak, depression, sadness, abuse, trauma, loss, all my pain and suffering. But in reflection Alcohol, you have brought much more bad than good, and I want my life back.

While under your influence I have,

•Hurt those I loved both verbally and physically

•Cheated, lied, stolen, and destructed

•Put myself in countless irresponsible situations

•Driven my car and almost killed myself

•Lost friends that meant a lot to me

•Exposed my body to disgusting drooling men

•Had sex with strangers

•Embarrassed myself countless times

•Ruined job opportunities

You have clouded my mind, so I couldn't see things clearly.

I have lost so much precious time in this short life, recovering from spending time with you–

I am done.

I will give you some time to process all of this information, but whether you understand or not this is how it is going to be for the next 6 weeks.

It is goodbye for now, until I am ready to see you again.

I will see you when I see you.

With Love,

Sterling

Karma's a Bitch

by Lyra Hawthorne

She was acting weird–
My best friend

The minute I hung up the phone
I knew something was wrong

*"Meet me at Cannons Grille for a drink.
I need to talk to you."*

It was a bar we never went to
An older crowd
A place we wouldn't run into anyone we knew

My heart was in my throat
My stomach was in knots
I knew shit was about to get real

I just had no idea
            how real

Small talk and pleasantries
Beers ordered and cigarettes lit

That's when Tonya walked in–

It was always the three of us together
We were inseparable
Why didn't she say Tonya was coming?

That's when it hit me–
Before the words even escaped her lips
Tonya grabbed a beer and lit a smoke then
it was back to the pleasantries

"Can you guys please tell me what is going on?"

But I already knew the answer…

The story goes:
That my bestie's boyfriend hooked up with our friend–

She was a slut
A slut I refuse to name because
She doesn't deserve the recognition

I was gripping the side of the booth
I was praying that was all she was going to tell me
But my gut knew better

This said slut also had sex with my boyfriend

The reason she knew was because
she caught her boyfriend in a lie, and he confessed

that he cheated
My boyfriend fucked her the following weekend at a party, and
he knew because he was also there

He saw it with his own eyes
all while he was cheating on her again

"We sure know how to pick em, huh!"

The worst part–

All our friends had already heard this story

I was the last one to know

Silence washed over the table
I was out of my body
I felt my ears catch fire
My chest was constricting

How had everyone smiled in my face for so long?
They knew the truth and didn't tell me

All the sounds around me amplified
yet somehow, they drowned out the noise

I could see her mouth moving
but my world had fallen into a haunting silence

Every naive ounce of trust I gave him was in vain
Everything that I thought was real
for the last four years was a lie

I wanted to be his wife–
We had already picked out our children's names
We had fucking plans

She took everything from me

He–
He had fucking betrayed me

My mind drifted on the way home…
He was barely working
He would play video games in my bedroom while I was working
and going to college full time

No one was paying rent—
My mother was buying us groceries

I wanted more
I wanted us to take the next step—
To get our first apartment
For him to have ambition
A better job
A higher education
A fucking credit score

I really wasn't happy

In that moment I was so blindsided
A plethora of memories flooded into my mind
That stupid Kenny Rogers CD he played in my car on the way
home from our first date

The sound of his laugh
The way it felt when he put his hand on my face
and kissed me
Laughing for hours
Dancing all alone at the end of the night

It was always just us in our own little world
The innocence we shared
The deep connection we had

The unbelievable sexual chemistry
It was a love that may never be matched
A love I would be forced to say goodbye to

"Hey!"
"Hey…"

I snapped back to reality

I just wanted to be alone

I slammed three beers and kissed the girl's goodbye
We had all had enough for one night
I sat in the car and cried
I was not prepared to face the music

I threw up in the parking lot

What I didn't know was that the universe was silently preparing
my revenge–

And oh how sweet
that shit would be

I wiped my tears and dragged my rolling travel bag of college
books into the house

The sounds of Call of Duty and Entertainment Tonight told me I
was home

I said hi to mom–
I gave her the *'I'm not ok but I'll tell you later' look*

I took a shower to buy myself some time
The water was boiling hot
It burned terribly but I couldn't move
I just needed something to hurt
To hurt worse than the pain
that just ripped through my heart

Reality was starting to slowly creep in–
Ready to take full hold of my sanity

Confronted
Denied
Exposed

I was determined to find the truth
Phone records printed and highlighted
I called every witness to the stand
I couldn't eat
I couldn't sleep
I couldn't hear another fucking apology

I wouldn't have known where she lived if I wouldn't have
accidentally ended up at her house weeks prior

It was an unexpected girl's pool day
She had no idea I was coming
Not that day—

And not today

I was hysterical
We had a huge fight
Sleep deprived
I was running on pure adrenaline–
Fueled by alcohol and rage

I raced to her house
I was going to beat the shit out of that bitch
I needed someone to take my aggression out on–

Someone who I could fight
because I couldn't fight him.

I banged on the front door like the fucking FBI
I was screaming and yelling–
Threatening and laughing like a lunatic

Kicking the door
Slamming my hands on the siding

She didn't answer
Smart girl
I probably would have killed her

I tried for months—
But I just couldn't do it

I couldn't look at him the same
I couldn't believe a word he said
Everything he did was a turn off

He was too comfortable
Overweight
A mean shitty drunk

I was just done

One morning I woke up and something snapped
Something changed

I don't even know what it was but it was time

I wanted him out of my bed—
Out of my house
Out of my life

He was going to pay for the lies and betrayal
I had never felt this level of pain before

I would cry for hours—
Those loud bellowing cries
Like someone was ripping my heart from my chest
Beyonce "*If I were a boy*" was my mantra

We had a fight that morning
We were eating a nice Sunday breakfast with my mom

I threw my plate in the sink–
"GET OUT GET OUT GET OUT!"

I ripped his clothes out of the closet
"HERE I'LL HELP YOU!"

Everything I had been holding inside tore its way out of me like
a caged fucking animal

I called an emergency meeting
My bestie met me at the corner store

Our friend had called earlier and asked
if we wanted to go on the boat

I couldn't have been happier
It was time to go drink this shit away
I needed a mental break
I had been a head case for months

I needed to forget–
Just for a day

The timing was impeccable!
Thank you, dear revengeful universe

I was about to get mine

He was tall
Tan
Had a beautiful smile

He was in college
He had plans
He was buff
Bodybuilder buff
And he couldn't keep his eyes off me…

It was an instant connection

We were so into each other
We drank all day
We fucked all night

I knew the next day things were going to be different
I didn't want to delete the pictures
from Sunday Funday

I didn't want to forget the new smell
on my t-shirt

I wanted to feel happy again
This would do the trick just fine

Boy did it ever–

It was the best summer of my life
My ex was crying at work mowing lawns

A well-deserved pain

He cracked me a beer
He lit me a fresh smoke
He tilted my chin up to kiss me
He sat his tan chiseled body next to mine

This overwhelming sense of contentment took hold as I rested
my hand on his leg

The boat motor was whirring
Drowned out by Five Finger Death Punch
The wind in my hair
The waves splashed up on my arms
The sunset was beautiful

I was happy

I felt like myself again
My real self

For the first time in months

I took a long swig of beer
I put my sunglasses on
A satisfying smirk crept onto my lips…

Karma's a Bitch

The Move
by Margaret Belvedere

My living situation had become strained—
The tension with my neighbors was palpable
After his drunken rage and threats
I was politely asked to leave

I couldn't afford it anyway
I never could afford it in the first place

It was my mistake from the beginning—
At least that's what I told myself

He was my way out
My *escape*
and he knew it

It was all a part of his plan
He was already in

covert control

I didn't want things to go down this way—
But I had to go

On one side of the coin
Insurmountable relief
I didn't have to work 7 days a week anymore
I could breathe again

On the other side of the coin—
The signs were right in front of me
like neon billboards and bright city lights

But my eyes were closed

The move was hellacious
I had to pack up my entire apartment alone
The dreams of my new life were being crushed
right in front of my very eyes

Every step of the way was another issue
Another dramatic scene
I was stressed beyond belief
I was forced to move forty miles south

It was a far cry from my original plan
for my move to California

It was a commute that used to take me
four minutes would now take an hour each way

I had seventy-two hours to be out
I had never even seen the place that
I was about to call home

I shouldn't have gone
I should have negotiated with the landlord

I should have called my dad

Instead
I lied to him

This was the first lie of many
I didn't want to admit I failed
I didn't see any other way out

I was already brainwashed

It was too late

It was the beginning of my downfall

but the real spiral
was just

around

the corner

The Last Drop
by La Browne

I was pacing around–
Counting down the minutes
until he walked through the door

I never knew what to expect
I never knew what version of him was going to arrive

It was agonizing
and he was late–
This was confirmation my night would be hell

Faking it for my kids was taking its toll

Mentally
Physically
Emotionally

I was exhausted
I was sick of wearing my mask
The mask that bore a permanent smile
yet on the inside I was dying

"Come on, it's time for bed."

My babies were fed
Cleaned
Tucked in–
A melatonin prescribed for an extra level of protection

I sat on the edge of her soft pink comforter running my fingers
through her hair sending her off to a safe place

I prayed my baby girl was fading
into some kind of beautiful dream

Only I was strong enough for this nightmare—
At least that's what I told myself

It was past 11pm
I had to close my eyes
Dread was consuming me
I knew he was coming

The slam of the front door
jolted me from my temporary sanity

Before I could even lift my head
He was next to me

I could smell his wrath
He was seeping tequila
His words cut into my soul
His eyes looked right through me

Fear surged through my body

"Please don't wake my babies."

As long as they were safe
I didn't care what he was going to do to me

He began pushing me—
Forced me out of bed and out of the bedroom

"Why didn't you answer the phone, you piece of shit?"

"I was stuck at the gas station."
"Cops were following me—You were too busy sleeping!"

"I didn't get any calls from you. Look."

I showed him my phone to try and calm him down
I prayed he would just pass out
I prayed this nightmare would be over–
But that was not in the cards tonight

"We can talk about this tomorrow. Let's go to sleep."

His face twisted with rage

"FUCK YOU!"
"You're a shitty two-faced bitch!"

He started throwing things
He screamed and yelled louder and louder
My insides were churning
I dodged baby wipes and house plants

I could hear my baby girl starting to stir and whimper
"I am done with you. We are going to get rid of you."

I screamed and I yelled
I matched his crazy

Throwing my fake mask off once and for all
I was done with his shit
I was a monster now too

A monster he created

I needed to think–
To buy myself some time

I pretended to use the bathroom but now
I was trapped

He was blocking me from getting out
When I finally looked up at him—

He was holding a pair of scissors
My heart dropped

This is it
He is going to kill me

I was scared for my life—
But I had to keep a level head for my children
I would protect them at all costs

I chose to look unfazed
I washed my hands instead to distract him—
Just long enough to redirect his attention

He started to use the bathroom
I saw my chance

I ran

My daughter's cries came back into focus
I rushed to her

Things had reached a new level of fucked
and I needed to get us to safety

She was gripping my neck so tight
I could hardly breath

She was so tired and confused
She was only two years old

My love for her drowned out his threats
My adrenaline rejected the pain

He was punching my feet
Hitting my ankles with his car keys

My lack of response sent him over the edge

He jumped on me and tried to
pry my daughter from my arms

She didn't want to go with him
She was screaming
Fight or flight had taken full control

The fear was gone
The will to survive had taken the driver seat
I held on to my daughter tight
His weight was on top of me
Her screams were piercing my eardrums
My maternal instinct pushing through the pain
I tried to call 911
He threw my phone

I couldn't move

I used the last card I had to play
I screamed to my son for help

"911 what's your emergency?"
"My parents are fighting. My mom is calling for help!"
"What is your address, son?"
"I don't know."

His rage turned to the 911 operator–

"Yeah, tell them your parents are fighting!!!"
"I'll give you the address! COME ON OVER!"

He retreated to the kitchen
I had a moment to get my bearings
My phone back in hand
911 redialed
"You're safe. There are already deputies outside."

I ran–
My saviors were waiting outside that front door
He was cuffed
I let out a sigh of relief
They took him in
My nightmare was finally over

What I didn't realize was the path of healing would be so much
harder than what I had been through

I fled my home
My job
My college education

He took everything
My choices
My opinions
My friends
My freedom
My happiness
My whole life

For twelve long years I agreed with him

I soaked in the moments he was away
I took the invisible punches to avoid the real ones
My only objective was to protect my children

I withered away behind my fake mask

My kids were my strength
They were my only way to cope
I focused on church, prayer, and positive thinking–
Being a good person and doing the right thing
I found solace in my family, my therapy groups,

and God

The sense of relief that washed over me
It was indescribable
I was finally free

free of pain
and free to heal

For anyone who is still in the throes of abuse
I urge you to make hard choices
I urge you to leave your home and start over–
Or violence will choose a path for *you*

Know that you are not alone and on the other side–
There is insurmountable relief

Freedom

There is an opportunity to feel like yourself again
and above all else

happiness

Harsh Winter
by Anonymous

Have my words ever meant anything to you?

Do our conversations leave a note in your mind?

A constant reminder like the ones in my room,
sticky notes filled with positive thoughts
reminding myself to be present.

Words of affirmation,

words you have
never said.

Do you ever think of me?
Not because you have to but because you want to?

I will never really know you.
You have never let me in–
You don't know how to tell the truth.

I think of your mind as a forest

in the depths of winter.

Heavy snowfall covering the ground and the trees,

footprints in the snow the only indicator

of my presence,

slowly getting smaller

disappearing

as if I was never born.

I like to think that
maybe I will find answers here.

The moon reflecting off the shimmering snow

casting some light onto why you went

through with having me,
despite not wanting me.

Did I disgust you so much that you couldn't

even decide what to call me?

Did you just open a random book
and choose a name?

One you didn't even like...

Maybe here, I'll find out why you were

so disappointed

that I was a girl.

Maybe here,

I'll find out why everything else was

more important than your child.

Maybe here,

I'll find out why you love my brother

more than you love me

and why
I can't do anything to please you.

I wish I knew you

but I will only ever know

the *impact* of me

and how much it hurts that I am still here.

But my footprints won't be around forever Mom,

they never stay

    for very long.

When the spring rolls around
and the snow melts,

I will go with it.

One day soon the spring will come,

    and you will no longer have to endure

      this harsh winter.

The Mustard Stain

by Margaret Belvedere

We were finally settled into our new place
Me, three Marines, a guy on the couch
and my five-pound Chihuahua

There were automatic rifles on the walls
Heavy metal blaring through the surround sound
Pool table in the garage

It was the definition of a Bachelor pad

No personal space
No closet space
I was just a guest in this house

The night was young
The boys were lubed up–
Ready to go chase some tail

It was the perfect setup for a date night in
Movies, wine, and popcorn

I was ecstatic

Jazz on the record player
We ate another incredible dinner
The house peaceful for once

Kitchen cleaned
Wine poured
Movie started
Time to snuggle up

In a quick flash—
My entire reality was redefined
His mask was about to come off
I had been captured...
A rare bird in a cage

Now I was trapped with no escape
and he knew it

The entire coffee table shattered
The living room floor was covered in glass

My wine streamed down the white walls
like blood

Everything in proximity was
smashed and destroyed

He retreated to the bedroom
with a handle of liquor
in a rage

I was in complete shock
I sat in silence for a moment

What in the actual fuck just happened?

The writing was dripping down the walls

Instead of deciphering the message
I did the only thing I knew how to do—
Clean up the mess

Little did I know this was only the beginning Cleaning up the
broken pieces would become a daily occurrence

I tried to console him
Impossible

He was battling demons
Intoxicated
Pointless

Why?
I continued to ask him

"There's a fucking mustard stain on my couch."

If I had just seen the stain before—
Would this have happened?
How did I miss this?
Could I have prevented this?

The answers didn't matter
His mask was going to come off
Sooner or later

I was already locked in his cage

His claws were in
too deep

Moronica
by Veronica Christina Gonzalez

Once there was a little girl
her heart was filled with joy

Her mothers heart filled with lust and greed
The need for attention
The need to always in the spotlight

The girl had to hide her heart
If she let her light shine her mother would get
envious
and the little girl would pay the price

When she was bullied at school–
Her mother would join in

When she repeated a naughty word–
Her mother would slap her

Her birthday gift that year - food thrown in her face
Her mother laughed
while she cried

The child support was spent
keeping the liquor cabinet full
while the little girls stomach remained
empty

The mother bribed the neighbors with
drinks in exchange for money

and access

to the little girl's
bedroom

Lustful for young blood
fulfilling their needs
in her age 6-9 little girl's
cotton briefs

Then the mother was pregnant again—
Another mouth she couldn't feed

She was tormented and taken advantage of
The little girl attempted suicide
She was unsuccessful

Screaming and yelling
Violence and abuse
Provocative remarks and police sirens
are the only things she had ever known

Years of abuse continued—
The little girl was beaten
while her mother sat there and watched

"Fat Pig."
"Idiot."

The most common—
"Moronica"

A beautiful blend between moron
and her name, Veronica.
Thus - Moronica
This is what the little girl's name would be...

The laughter of her mother and her boyfriend
ripped at her soul

tearing her down
further
and
further
then she could even grasp

Moronica had no friends
She did poorly in school
She couldn't focus

She was bullied for smelling bad
For not taking care of herself
When she was on her menstrual cycle–
She didn't know what to do
Her mother never showed her how

The Mother hated Moronica
She would harass the little girl
She pushed her to her limits

She recorded only the parts that made her look bad
Painting a false picture of the girl in order to deceive

She was out of control
Unmanageable
Belligerent!

Moronica needed to go to Juvenile Hall
A plan to get rid of her once and for all

But the mother's plan backfired

As the little girl loved juvenile hall
She loved the staff, having a warm meal
and peace in her heart
even if it was
for just a moment

Clueless as to why she was there–
Moronica soaked in this newfound feeling of safety
The mother quickly caught on to this

Moronica was
not allowed
to be happy

The mother was vicious and vindictive
locking her out of the house
on a blistering hot summer day

She knew the little girl would act out
and she could get everything on camera

It was the perfect setup to execute her plan

Overheated
Banging on the door
Screaming and yelling
The mother spewed insults–
She broke her spirit into even smaller pieces

Moronica got the courage to take her phone away
The mother grabbed her by her hair–
Spitting in her face

Moronica was desperate to end the pain and suffering
She grabbed a kitchen knife

She threatened to kill herself
Throwing things
Breaking windows
She couldn't take this anymore

The mother saw her golden opportunity
An actress overnight
She was the victim
and Moronica was out of control

The police arrived
Moronica stepped in front of the judge

She was deemed *"Guilty except for insanity"*

The mother moved out of state

The father turned his eye
He was ashamed
Embarrassed
He disowned her

Her sisters were too young to understand

Moronica was sent away
Sentenced: Up to five years
in The Children's Farm Home Facility

Abandoned
Alone
Soon to be
forgotten

Sam
by Kennedy Blum

Fantasizing
about the man you were
for a fraction of the time
before you acted so unforgivable
and then forced me
to forgive you

Fantasizing
about that inner child
that was so tender
and so easy
to love
before that monstrosity
would take his place

Fantasizing
about the life
where you gave me everything
if I could just shut the fuck up
and be what you wanted

Fantasizing
about the post-fight love making
where the apologies were so real
and for a moment we could live in this world
without you destroying it

The Deception
By Margaret Belvedere

He paid all the bills
Every dollar I made at the bar–
I was to give to him when I returned home

He called it...

'His walking around money'

He broke everything that meant something to me He broke
EVERYTHING
He made me feel worthless–
But at the same time the luckiest girl in the world

The emotional warfare was immeasurable

He forced me to get joint bank accounts
Joint car insurance

As soon as we were both on my insurance–
Someone stole parts off his car
He filed an insurance claim
It was a lie
We got a check

He lied about his job
He stole from Camp Pendleton
He had an ex-wife

Christmas eve meant the world to my mother–
It was, and still is the most important
day of my year

He wouldn't let me go home for the holiday
to see my family because
"we" couldn't afford to go

I talked to them for five minutes on Christmas Eve in the alley
behind the bar I worked at
before he made me hang up the phone
and have Christmas Eve dinner
at the Harbor House Café

My heart was aching

His omelet was runny–
Torment and rage consumed him

Jesus Christ it was just a fucking omelet!

I drank beers as fast as I could
I was beside myself
My mother cried that night
I was holding back my own tears

Deep Breaths
He will pay for this

He was starting to take real things from me

Time... precious time–
Time I could never get back

Anger and resentment were beginning to build

My demeanor was shifting
Something dark was lurking inside of me–
Waiting to surface

My bestie from home was visiting in the spring

When we planned the trip
excitement was at an all-time high

Just two single girls lying on the beach
soaking in the sun
soaking in my beautiful new life

I took time off work–
Time I couldn't afford to take
He convinced me to use my
Lowe's credit card to buy flowers and mulch
and a gazebo

'We can't have guests with the yard this way'

I cleaned and prepared everything
I couldn't wait for her to land!

From the moment she arrived–
Her trip was a living nightmare

Instead of enjoying our time we had to
tiptoe around his mood
Everything we did was on his terms
This was not the vacation we had planned

He got drunk and crashed my car
while we were all sleeping

In retrospect I'm confident it was on purpose
We were going to drive to Vegas the next day

It was supposed to be a surprise–
A surprise he couldn't wait to ruin
He woke me up at 7am wasted
Accusing me of kissing his friend

False

I was barely awake and already seeing red
I chucked a beer bottle–
It shattered on the wall
He smashed my big screen TV on the floor
Stomping on it until it was destroyed

He ripped the shelfs off the walls
Broke picture frames
Door frames

We broke everything in that bedroom
Screaming
Fist fighting
Demolishing
I was becoming the monster

I packed my bags
I took my bestie
The guy on the couch
and my dog

I brushed my teeth and
changed my clothes at a rest stop
This was a new low…

I did the only thing I knew how to do–

I drank through it
pushing reality away,
and I still paid for a rental car
and got us to Vegas the next day.
The Plot was thickening
My rage was building

One day I came home,
and my tiny boy was all beat up–
His eye was bulging from the socket

I had never felt this level of pain in my heart seeing his sweet
little body so thrashed

"It was an animal attack."

He said it was because
I left him in his pen in the backyard

My gut knew otherwise

$700 vet bill
My mother paid because we were so broke

Because
*"HE SPENT ALL
OF
OUR
MONEY"*

Three days later my sweet Lamb ran away
still in his cone of shame

I was in agonizing pain
I failed him

I was supposed to protect him
It was my only job

I looked for him for weeks
door to door
shelter to shelter

He was gone

I lied to my mother
She thought he was still alive
I just didn't have the heart to tell her
That was her boy
She called him Son

It was one of the hardest things
I have ever done in my life.
Every time I would get off the phone with her—

I would sob

Things were getting darker
The fights worse
The bruises bigger
The misery was consuming

I wanted to die

After a long sober talk one day we decided—
It was time to move

A fresh start
A new beginning
Close to work again
I told myself
everything was going to be ok

Things were better for a while...
We finally had our own place
The hydrocodone kept him busy
House clean
Dinner always on the table

Stevie Ray Vaughan records
filling the house with calm romantic vibes

My pajamas laid out when I got home from work
My work clothes clean and folded–
Laid out beautifully in the morning along with my coffee and
breakfast

My wine glass filled and on my end table
before my ass even hit the couch
Things were okay
I felt a glimmer of hope
That's when he asked me to marry him...

Once I had a ring on my finger
one that he convinced me to co-sign for–

Everything changed

After visiting home
Meeting each other's families
Doing the whole song and dance
Guest lists - dress shopping

Fucking Pinterest Inspo

The violence, lies, and abuse only amped up

It was a bad night–

Too much booze
Too many pills

I was butt naked
Cold steel in my hand
I shoved the gun in his mouth
He was on his knees
He begged me to do it

I screamed at the top of my lungs
and pulled the trigger–
I wish it would have been loaded

Although I wouldn't have the freedom
to share this story if that was the case…

I collapsed in exhaustion
Hysterical
Things had reached a new level of fucked

On my Birthday–
He staged a break-in at our apartment

Everything was broken
It was traumatizing

I didn't know until later that it was his doing–
He even wrote a message on the bathroom mirror
like he always did
just to break it
so it looked believable

I left work early
I was late to my own party
In complete in disarray
putting on my fake face

one I knew all too well
An insurance claim filed
It was a lie
We got a check

He would rip the doors off the hinges in rage–
Break banisters and put holes in the walls
Then just slip the handyman a $20
Poof!
It was like nothing ever happened

He had a snake's tongue
He walked on water

And then…
He got dishonorably discharged
from the US Marine Corp

A new episode of my fucked-up life
was about to unfold

I was thrust back into working seven days a week
My nightmare returned
I was back to square one
Two Jobs
Punching the time clock at
9am and ending at 2am - 7 days a week
He was depressed and broken
no motivation
He didn't know what to do for work
Suddenly his addiction to painkillers
had reached a breaking point

He always took them because he was
injured in combat–
That was his excuse

The lie he told me
The lie he told himself

One day he stumbled into my work
Jeans were ripped - wearing weird Velcro shoes
*'He was hit on the freeway by a car
on his motorcycle'*
but somehow managed
to go to the store to buy shoes?

More like he swerved in front of a car
on the freeway

so he could manage to get

more
pain killers

I don't even know how he got there
I was beyond embarrassed

We spent two days in the hospital
I had to pretend to be his wife Alica
to show face for his Sargent

I was blindsided–
in complete shock
He was still married

I felt like someone punched me in the gut

Everything I thought I knew
was a fucking lie.

Everything was out of control
The Morphine intake was on another level
I can still see the clouded look in his eyes
I can hear his fake screams of being in pain
Just so the nurses would give him another push
Itching and scratching constantly
Yelling and cursing at the staff
Sneaking out to smoke every fifteen minutes

It was a fucking nightmare

All for attention and more pain meds
I was at the end of my rope
I couldn't do this anymore

I was living in hell
He watched my every move
He was around every corner–
Texting me constantly

I was working two jobs and we were so broke
Scared every month that we wouldn't make rent
Scared there would be
an eviction notice on our door

He spent money faster than I could make it
There were constant alerts on my banking app
Withdrawal from ATM–
Bar Tab
Bar Tab
Bar Tab
Withdrawal from ATM

Guinness and Jameson shots
until
he was blind

The emotional warfare was consuming me
I was drowning

He would do something horrific
and then leave a diamond necklace in my car
or send a dozen roses to my work

all on my dime

One day he sent me to the spa
He went in person to make the appointment
He told everyone that I was his wife
blowing that *American Psycho* smoke
up their asses

When I arrived–
They were all talking about
what a charming and incredible husband I had

It was gut wrenching and sickening
playing the part
I threw up in the bathroom before my service
I was becoming physically ill

Psoriasis had covered my body
but I was too busy covering up my bruises
and pretending that I was okay to face it,
I just drank more instead

I told no one
I lied to everyone
I was withering away

I didn't even know who I was
or who was looking back at me
in the mirror anymore
I was lost–
Completely broken
I didn't know how much more I could take

That's when I found out that he cheated on me

It was like a bomb exploded my insides
I was informed of this information
after I had been day drinking
with friends for hours
No way to see clearly
No way to process what I just learned–

Excellent

I was crushed beyond belief
That was the last thing I was expecting
Although I should have expected it

Stupid
Blind
Embarrassed

That was his breaking point
He was about to go off the deep end

I reached for something to hold on to
but the steady place I once had
slipped through my fingers like smoke

I was desperately lost

Alcohol
by Kennedy Blum

Don't you want to
live?

Don't you want to see me
have kids?

Don't you want to
watch me age?

Don't you want to
get to the next stage?

Is getting blackout drunk every night really that much more
important than having a relationship with your daughter?

Fight harder

Motherhood
by Gina Artiglio

The sterile smell of antiseptic filled my nose
The humming of the machines was loud
The ache in my heart was louder
The white walls closing in on me

A nurse emerged through the curtain
"Would you like to hold him?"
I couldn't breathe

Even now I can feel his tiny body
in my arms
still

I was sobbing
Inconsolable
an empty crib in the corner
a painful reminder
of where he was supposed to be

Alive
cooing and crying
keeping me up all night

I brushed his soft hair
He looked just like Justin
My first born
I was alone
There was no one there to take my pain away

How am I going to handle this?
Everyone is going to ask me where the baby is
I just had a baby shower
My heart wretched in pain

I screamed and yelled
Flailing in my bed
Ripping at my c-section wound
Bleeding
Feeling nothing
Crying out in agony

They quickly moved me as to not disturb the new mothers as
they were relishing
 in the joy *of*
   Motherhood

I was physically ill
There was an immediate void
A void no number of tears could fill
I wanted to die
He slipped through my fingers like grains of sand

I was shattered

I met Kenny when I was in my early 20's
He was a Marine
I was a preschool teacher by day
A waitress by night
My parents loved him and he loved me

We were staying in California after he was discharged

He had a security job
We did alright
But I wanted more
A better life
and I was going to get it
I saved enough to buy a house
We moved in together

A new home
A new car
A new life
I was the breadwinner

We had dogs and cats
A whole family of puffer fish
We were happy

But I always saw myself
as a mom

I craved it
I knew that motherhood was my purpose
I wanted a full house
Kenny was on board
We couldn't wait to get to work
We tried for 8 months

Nothing
I was stressed
Discouraged
Disappointed

Finally–
A positive pregnancy test
God told me it was going to be a boy

His name
Justin

Holding him in my arms for the first time was
Indescribable
That moment transcended words–
It was a profound sense of awe and wonder

A piece of my heart made flesh

I traced his delicate features with trembling fingers
marveling at the miracle I held in my hands
I had been dreaming of this day for so long it was more
beautiful than I ever could have imagined

Six months later my wildest dreams came true
Kenny graduated nursing school and got a job
I could officially stay home with my baby

I was elated
and ready to try
for more

We tried
and tried
and tried

Finally
I was pregnant
four months later

I wasn't

I woke up this particular morning
and took a test like I did every morning

There were boxes in bulk under our bathroom sink
same old same old but today—
It was positive

I took a long deep breath
Tears streamed down my face
I was elated

I cried and cried and cried for months

A few months was all I got
I started spotting I knew something was wrong
I could feel it

The pain was so intense
The cramps gripping my abdomen with a ferocity that felt like it
was tearing me apart from the inside out–

Because it was

Every contraction was a harsh reminder of the life that was
growing in me quickly slipping away

    in a cascade of
      blood and tissue

The pain I could handle
The emotional agony I could not
That cut the deepest

I was sobbing uncontrollably
clutching my stomach
grief and loss were suffocating me

A gut-wrenching sorrow washed over me
I felt a profound sense of betrayal
both from my body
and the universe
or God

Whoever or whatever is out there
was ripping my heart out of my chest

What did I do wrong?

I was consumed by guilt and shame

emptiness

My dreams of a family continued to be shattered
into a million jagged pieces

I was hollow

I sat there staring at the blood-stained tiles below my feet as
loneliness cut to the core of my being

I was isolated
in a sea
of grief

I felt discouraged and sad
but I wasn't giving up

I was determined
I wanted a big family
Maybe that baby just wasn't meant for me

We will try again
Everything is going to work out
I believed it to be true
Little did I know it was a lie
Just a lie I told myself

A lie to keep going
A lie that would continue to bring me heartache

I decided if I was broken
If my body wasn't going to do what it was supposed to
that I would adopt–
But we didn't stop trying

I went through all the paperwork
The interviews
The long hours on the phone
The planning and preparation

In just two months I would have another baby
Even if it wasn't mine by blood
I would love him or her just the same

And then—
A miracle
Another positive test
This was it I could feel it

I was so excited to give Justin a biological sibling
A brother

Everything was finally working out
I had a wonderful pregnancy
I couldn't wait to meet him

His name
Kasey

After much thought I chose to put a pause on the adoption
process to allow myself to relish in this moment

A moment
I was longing for
dreaming of

A moment that would prove
to once again be *brief*
It was an indescribable feeling—
When I held him in my arms for the first time
Pure magic

An instant connection
It was coursing through my entire being
My heart expanding with a love
so fiercely that it took my breath away

His button nose
His tiny eyelashes
A living breathing miracle

This was worth all the struggles
All the tears
All the stress and sacrifice
The sheer perfection
We were bonded
Nothing else mattered

And then
once again
my world
came
crumbling down

The doctor gave me a shot so I could get some sleep
I needed rest but I didn't want to sleep
I wanted to be with my baby

I was resistant but listened
to my doctor's recommendation

While I slept Kasey passed away
I would never hear his cries again

Time stopped

A whirlwind of emotions gutted me
The phantom weight of him in my arms remained

The sterile hospital
The empty crib
The deafening sounds

of silence

Everywhere I went–
"Where's the baby?"

Those words shredded my insides
I couldn't bear to explain why he wasn't with me

I didn't want to live
I didn't want to answer anyone's stupid questions

To top it all off
I was denied an autopsy
Forever in the dark

Never knowing
what took his last breath

The loss of Kasey took everything from me
When reality finally sank in
the world was tilted off its axis

I was stranded in a place of pain and confusion
A deep profound ache stemmed from my core
An overwhelming sense of emptiness
A piece of my heart torn away

Guilt gnawed at me
What could I have done differently?
How could I have done better?

I replayed every moment of my pregnancy
searching for signs I may have missed
desperate for some explanation

Some reason to make sense
of the senselessness

Why?

So many other women didn't want kids
I so desperately wanted a family

What was wrong with me?

Justin was the only thing keeping me afloat
He was my only coping mechanism
Even if I was broken I still had to be a mom

I threw myself into motherhood to give Justin the best life
possible and to love him unconditionally everyday

I didn't want to give up
I dug deep to keep the faith

I kept the excitement and anticipation alive imagining children's
laughter filling our home
Tiny fingers clinging to mine

Each passing month eagerly awaiting the news
of a positive pregnancy test

Our hopes still soaring at the possibility
of a new life coming into ours–
But as time went on and months turned into years

Hope slowly started to give way replaced with

frustration and despair

Each negative pregnancy test a crushing blow
A reminder of a dream that was just out of reach

Didn't God see it?
Didn't he understand that I wanted to be a mom?

We kept trying
I kept crying
My tears were unstoppable
I was scared
I didn't know how to carry on
The constant flashbacks of that hospital room
haunted me

"Would you like to hold him?"

I can still hear her words
crisp as the day she said them

There was only one answer in my mind
We had to keep trying

The Doctors said I needed pills to conceive
I didn't want them
I wanted to do this on my own
I was stubborn
I would have the family I wanted
I was determined
Kenny was supportive
We kept at it
I am not sure if anyone can really relate to me
I think differently than most
I would not give up

No matter the pain
The suffering
We would keep trying

We would keep believing in the possibility of more children—A
sibling for Justin

The joy of a new baby
It was all I could think about

I refused the setbacks
They would not define me
I drew strength from the love of my partner

I became hypersensitive to the rhythms of my body listening to
the whispers and cues

A newfound sense of clarity and intuition
increasingly aware of the chances

A chance of
successful
fertility

Embarking on this journey once again
I allowed myself to feel hope
Warmth and anticipation
To imagine what she would be like
This time I knew she was going to be
a girl
Five months later she was gone too
I had to have a D&C to remove the fetus

My spirit was broken
I was dealing with so many emotions
I wanted to give up but I couldn't

No amount of pain could stop me from having a family

A few months later we had another positive test
I could feel it in my bones that this was it

I took 100 pregnancy tests
Two pink lines
Every morning
Every week
Every month
Just to be sure
Just a reminder that this was in fact *real*

Please God let this baby live
I thought that over and over in my head
Every single day

My heart was overflowing
with hope and boundless love

My doctor told me
"Don't be excited, this one will probably die too."

Even his words couldn't take my faith away

The day Makenna was born
was life or death for us both
I lost too much blood
She wasn't breathing
The doctors worked tirelessly
When I woke from surgery
I heard her cries for the first time and my heart burst
An overwhelming sense of love and joy consumed me

She was perfect

I marveled at her tiny delicate features
Her fluttering eyelashes
Her rosebud lips
Her tiny fingers holding onto mine

My eyes were brimming with awe
The weight of precious life resting on my chest
Love flooded my heart
Time stood still as I gazed upon my tiny *Miracle*

Makenna filled that baby feeling for a few years
and then she wasn't a baby anymore

It was a hard pill to swallow
The loss of Kasey still looming
The pain still very real

The white walls closing in on me
That nurse emerging through the curtain

"Would you like to hold him?"

Panic still sets in from time to time
I still smell that hospital
I can still hear that nurse's voice

I soak in every moment I have with my children
I have even started helping others who have been through
similar pain and suffering

Talking to friends on Facebook
and speaking at the Alano Club

My mother always taught me:
Be there for people no matter who they are

I want to make her proud God rest her soul

So I try to give back
I try to give the knowledge I have of pain and suffering
Helping others to find strength to keep their faith strong like
mine

Justin and Makenna
"Because of them I will not fail"

RIP Kasey 10/12/08
May you rest easy my lost loves:
2007 & Baby girl 2010

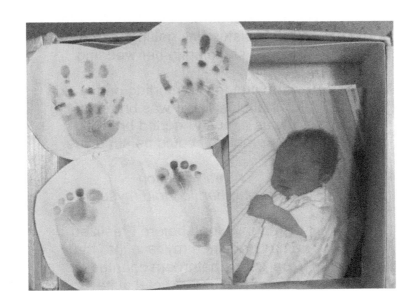

The Vacation
by Margaret Belvedere

Secrets Maroma Beach
His best friend from the Marine Corp
Adam's sister was getting married
He was standing in her wedding

The warm sun felt comforting on my skin
The crystal blue water was breathtaking
It was a much-needed break–
All our problems could be set aside

A real vacation
Just another lie I told myself

I tasted my blood before I realized
he had smashed my face into the
gorgeous bathroom counter
in our luxurious hotel suite

Another charge on my credit card
I was manipulated to make
The floor was covered in glass
My feet oozed red on the white marble

I grabbed my smokes
I ran

There was a tropical storm that night
The reception site was rained out

We were starving and too intoxicated before
we were served dinner

I danced at the reception
soaking in every moment of normalcy
as I waited for the devil to arrive

I ran across the entire property
The only place I knew to go was Adam's room

I was soaking wet–
running through a tropical storm soaking wet

I banged on the door
blood pooled at my feet
crusted in the corners of my mouth

My head was throbbing and starting to swell

No answer

I waited–
Bleeding and crying on the cold floor
A heap of broken abused women on the
pristine white marble

Pathetic

Adam comforted me and bandaged me up
We drank beers
We ordered medium rare steaks
with loaded baked potatoes
and four strawberry cheesecakes

It was three in the morning
I stayed with Adam until the sun came up
He was supportive
He explained a lot of things about the military
Just how broken he was

Not an excuse
but an explanation of the rage–
The uncontrolled emotions

I was finally starting to understand
the devil I knew

The next day at the pool
I lied
I told everyone I fell
walking back from the reception
It was a monsoon after all
It was slippery

My guts were turning
My face bruised

Lying had become so natural to me
I wanted to throw up
I did throw up
It was so easy for me to say
"Yeah I ate shit last night"
and laugh it off

The stress had taken such a toll
on my physical health
I looked like I had a disease
The amount of psoriasis I had on my body–
A leper
A beaten, broken-down leper

People stared at me in my bathing suit
I was beside myself.

He always looked at me
with such remorse
after a fight

He would console me
He would tend to my wounds
He would hold me and comfort me

The classic
fucked up
cycle of abuse

The emotional warfare
It was all starting to make sense–

War was all he knew

The Wash Bay
by Blanca Soto

Beep Beep Beep Beep!

The sound of the alarm clock
jolted me back to my harsh reality

Dread washed over me
I knew what I was facing
I knew I had to see him

I hung my head in my hands
mustering up every ounce of positivity
I could find within

I can't lose my job
I have to make it through this day without any issues
I just need to stay away from him

But my right to say "no" had already been taken away

I was an employee at an
environmental services company

I oversaw cleaning toilets
I already know what you're thinking

Real glamourous
It was a shit job

literally
But someone had to do it and I had bills to pay

My supervisor was a predator

He spewed vulgarity and lies about me
He lurked around every corner

He waited for his daily opportunity
to get me
alone

The moment I would clock in–
Sickness would wash over me
Fear and anxiety consumed me
A deep breath and a fake smile
I was just trying to survive

Head down
Cleaning supplies in hand
I would do everything in my power to stay invisible–
I'd avoid the all-male crew at all costs

I'd avoid the disrespectful conversations about women
Their sexual innuendos and rudeness and
with any luck I would avoid him

I was never lucky
Instead–I was taken advantage of

He would force himself on me
He would touch me inappropriately–
Reaching in my shirt
Grabbing at my breasts and nipples

He was a big man
I am a small woman

He overpowered me
He took what he wanted

If I didn't give him what he wanted–
I would face retaliation
He would speak to me like I was trash
criticizing my job performance
spreading nasty rumors about me being his lover

The sound of the laughter from the crew
ripped at my insides

I was an object
The agony was unbearable

The worst days were when he would take me offsite
He would pull me from the 'Wash Bay' and task me with
completing a cleaning job at a different location

where it was just the two of us

Fear would shrill through my body
Anxiety consumed me
The last time I had to go–
He locked himself in the bathroom with me
pushed himself on me and forcefully kissed me

My soul was tormented
I lived in a constant state of fear
I couldn't sleep
I was suffering in silence

The time came when I finally hit a breaking point
I was done surviving
I needed help

My roommate was my only real friend so I turned to her for support and advice

I was shattering
I couldn't live like this anymore

English is not my first language
She helped me write a letter
A letter explaining the sexual harassment
I was shaking when I gave it to my manager–

I prayed he would help me
I prayed my supervisor would be fired
I prayed this nightmare would be over
He didn't help at all
He promptly sent me to human resources

Human resources sent me right back to work with him like nothing ever happened

Betrayal and anger fought for first place
I wanted to disappear

One morning the manager called me into his office
He handed me a letter and with a quick signature
I was the one being removed
He got to stay

I was thrown into a whirlwind of emotions
I felt like I didn't matter

How am I being held responsible for his behavior?
Why am I guilty for telling the truth?

I wanted to dig a fucking hole and stick my head in it

My sister helped me get a lawyer
They didn't believe me and didn't help me
They held onto my funds
My suffering continued

Finally–
After informing the Bar Association of his actions
He was punished and my money was returned

My experience taught me valuable lessons
Most importantly I learned to value myself
*I will never let anyone under any circumstances disrespect me
ever again*

I am strong

I have the right–

The right to say

"No"

A Name
By Anonymous

I don't need you anymore

I'm finally ready to go

I've packed my bags

full of this resentment

I've washed away the salt from my skin—

The salt you poured on every one of my wounds

I am going to give myself a better life—

one without you in it,

calling me an asshole

poisoning me with your lies

I have no reason to stay

You have forgotten my name

Within that forgotten name

I have forgotten my meaning

You have forgotten

how much

You

tormented me

But I haven't forgotten

You

stripping me of a name–

Leaving me this cold shell of a person

Condescending stares

Silently telling me I'm worthless

Days you refused to look at me

the pain I constantly endured

All that remains between us is

the sweet gift of the gaslight

You are so talented,

even my memory has tricked me

into believing that

You

are the victim…

Instead of

Me

Free Standing Lamp
by Margaret Belvedere

This day was like any other—
We went out and got drunk

Shocker

I was so tired
Just trying to survive one more day
The walls had holes
Doors ripped off
A secret bank account

An escape plan
that lived only within the safety
of my mind

He got wasted and passed out in the car
on the way home

We were on PCH
so I decided
to go to the beach for a minute while he slept

"Happy" by Pharell Williams
was playing on the radio

I remember feeling the warm breeze on my face
but not getting out of the car
If he woke up and I wasn't there—
I would have been in trouble

I tried to sing along and feel happy
I just couldn't bring myself to be

That song will
haunt me forever

I had no idea what was coming
I wish I was more prepared—
But no one is prepared
to get assaulted
and seventy-two hours later

be homeless

When we got home he laid down on the couch
after calling me a whore
and continued to ruin my day

Per usual

I went to the porch to listen to music
and chain smoke
I was stressed
So fucking stressed

Thoughts raced
How do I get out of here?
I have no money

He has taken everything from me.
There is nowhere to turn
I'm a lost cause
I'm pathetic
I have nothing
I'm worthless
My Family is disappointed in me

I am right where he wants me
His precious caged bird

I just dominated another level of Candy Crush
when the front door came flying open
The free-standing lamp from the living room crashed onto the
sidewalk in front of me.

What the fuck is it now?

I threw my head back in the chair
I took one long deep breath
before I had to get in the ring
I hid my iPad in the grill for safety measures
and came through the front door

I was immediately hit with a picture
that he ripped off the wall
Glass shattered all over the floor
Blood streamed down my legs

He was destroying the house again

I grabbed my purse and keys
I tried to make it out the door
That's when he grabbed my laptop

My laptop was non-negotiable
NOT TO BE BROKEN
That was my lifeline
for work and our future.

SMASH

I lost it

I jumped on him and started swinging
He flipped me over and punched me
five times in the face

Everything was a blur

The next thing I knew—
There were people standing in our living room
There was a man screaming at him
to get off me and get out of the house
The woman helped me up
She helped me gather my things and
get them to my car

He was arrested and taken to jail

I still believe that that man and woman
were my grandparents coming to save me

I had never seen them before in my life
and I never saw them again after
The worst days of my life remained ahead of me
Our lease was up in a matter of days
My whole life was a piece of broken glass

So fragile
Barely existent
About to collapse
Traumatized
Abused and now

Homeless

Just a small nudge away from

full self-destruction

Innocence
by Loi'Alexis Siliuta

I rolled over in bed
mouth dry
head pounding
heart aching

It was 1:30 in the afternoon
I couldn't find the strength to get up or
the strength to move on or
the strength to get out of the depths of this despair

I was in the bowels of my darkest depression turning to the
bottle for comfort

Every night I was reminded
it was empty
like me

I had nothing left to give

I had condemned myself to isolation
No friends
No contact with the outside world

A disgusting cycle
of drinking to feel normal
then drinking to numb the pain

It was the 45th day of my self-inflicted sentence
I didn't know how much more my body could take
Tears streamed down my face as I lied in bed

"Babe I'm sorry but I am ready to go."
"It's ok, I know you are tired."

144

Our last words to each other echoing in my ears
repeating and repeating until I felt I was going mad

Flashbacks

Holding him in my arms
taking his last breath
I couldn't take it anymore
I was shattered

I grew up in Westminster, California
My parents were flawless–
They are still married to this day
I had a perfect example of how to live the right way

My dad was involved in the church
We lived next door to my grandma
We spent time together as a family
Mom, dad, and my three siblings

We shared a room and walked to school together
My life was perfect

I was shy and respectful
I did my chores and got perfect grades
I was always happy
I was saving myself for marriage
I would dream of the life I was going to have–
Working as a midwife or maybe with animals

The options were endless and I loved to dream
to imagine how beautiful things were going to be

I was eleven when everything changed
My entire life was thrusted into darkness

Plans derailed
My soul ripped apart
Leaving behind only pieces
Fragments of what I once was

In the wee hours of the night–
He stole my future
He stole my power

He stole my innocence

He was a family friend that stayed with us a week
It was his last night in town
He crept silently into our room–
Choosing between me and my younger sister

He held me down as I remained voiceless
struck silent

Not wanting my brother and sister
to witness this heinous act

When he was finished
I lied there silent
Tears filled my eyes
Agony filled my heart

I ran to my older sister's house
He was reported
I was showered

The police stopped him at the airport–
Moments shy of making his escape

I felt disgusting

I bleached every inch of our bedroom
I prayed the decontaminate would stop
The gnawing feelings growing inside of me

I was in denial and wildly uncomfortable
I was eleven and couldn't sleep without my parents

My life had been forever changed
I couldn't get it out of my head
I was physically ill
I felt vile

Many court dates later
Dragging out the pain
Suffering in silence
He plead guilty
He was sentenced to eight years–
But he had already sentenced me to life

I was just curious
the first time I swallowed that little pressed pill.

Sensations of warmth flushed my cheeks
spreading from my core

I was wrapped in a comforting embrace
Gentle waves of pleasure coursed through my body
There was a sense of lightness
It was pure euphoria

It was fucking sensational for just a minute
I didn't feel the pain anymore for just a minute
I wasn't obsessing about that night

for just a minute
I felt alive again

Curiosity turned to habit–
'Just for a minute' became just another day

I was unknowingly on a new path that would become

my prison

A path with *no escape*

I was ditching class and stealing from my parents
I was stealing from department stores
My grades were shit
I was constantly running away from home
I was constantly running away from myself

My parents were at the end of their rope
With no other options–
They sent me away

It was a really terrible punishment
I was sent to live with my favorite aunt and uncle
and my favorite three cousins in Kapolei on the beautiful
Hawaiian island of O'ahu

I loved it
Three or four months had gone by and everything was starting
to feel good again
and then I fucked up

I got in trouble
I got caught drinking

I was sent immediately back to the mainland
A ticket straight back to my distorted reality
I cried for days

It was my junior year of high school back in California
I started exploring my next curiosity–
Cocaine

Every fiber ablaze - vitality coursed through my veins
Colors sang - sounds danced
The world unfolded in brilliance

The canvas of my soul was brushed
with cocaine's sweet embrace

Each heartbeat orchestrating a symphony of pleasure
I felt alive

Beneath this euphoria lied the shadow of descent
I embraced fleeting immortality
I danced on the edge of oblivion

But the dance faded quickly–
Before I knew it the pain grew louder
Even cocaine wasn't enough to silence it

I was a runaway - motel to motel
I was gone for months

My parents were desperately chasing my whereabouts as I was
desperately chasing my high

This time it was meth

Just one thin line and the electric feeling can ignite every nerve
ending in your body –
It will send shivers of exhilaration along your spine
Your heart pounds like a jackhammer
Each beat synchronized with the rush of euphoria
Pulsing through your bloodstream

With each breath you feel invincible
Your senses heightened like a razor-sharp edge
as if the world itself bends to your will
After my last hard comedown and days of withdrawal
I had nothing left and no other choice
but to return home

My physical appearance had completely changed
I didn't know who was looking back at me
in the mirror anymore

I dropped out of school
I had taken a hard turn on my path of destruction—
Now I was facing a new challenge

I was pregnant

I sobered up and sustained the growing life inside
My beautiful baby boy
Things were hard but they were okay—
For a minute…

It seems to be a running theme in my life
Temporary happiness before the next bomb drops

I relapsed
My parents were caring for my son and then
his father was killed

Shot
Died in the ICU

I couldn't handle any more pain
I needed some solace
Out of nowhere—
In the quiet hum of a crowded room our eyes met

In that instant I felt the universe shift
Time stood still and amidst the chaos of life

I found peace in his presence
From that moment on
I knew I had found the missing piece of my soul

His name was Michael
Michael loved my son
We got serious fast
We were living with my parents
We were both struggling with drug addiction
Trying hard to do what was right–
But we didn't have to try hard to love each other

That's when my dance with alcohol began
It made me feel confident and happy
Not afraid to be myself
Never nervous and always up for conversation

Still…
I couldn't forget what he had done to me
I was just a little girl
There were tears that never ended

I hated him
I hated myself
I hated the world

I was in and out of rehab for years
Two stepping between sobriety and two more kids

A year went by
Michael was gone
I didn't see him
I didn't see my children

I wanted my man back
I wanted my family back
I did everything I could to get there
I got my shit straight–

A home, a car, a job
Michael came back to me

With his return the years of yearning dissolved
into his sweet embrace–

Destiny had finally woven our paths back together

I found the home I had been searching for in his arms
I felt hopeful for the first time

A few months later
he was diagnosed with Congestive heart failure

It was the beginning of the end for both of us

There were countless doctor visits
I had to quit my job

I gave up all my progress
But I would have done anything for Michael

My new job title:
Full time caregiver
Watching the man I loved
deteriorate

He was dying right in front of my eyes
I couldn't handle it
I couldn't cope
Not without alcohol anyway

I was watching him fade away and
my heart was breaking into a million pieces

Hospice was finally initiated
He died in my arms

"Babe, I'm sorry but I'm ready to go."
"It's okay, I know you're tired."

It had been a year
My soul was still broken but my heart was hopeful

I didn't want to give up on love

We met many years ago–
Fast friends

Always attracted
Always on drugs
Always making mistakes

His mistakes warranted a prison sentence

We reconnected
Snail mail and collect calls
It started off innocent but our connection grew
It grew into something I never could have imagined

I was loved and supported–
Even if it was from miles away

"For me, I often feel like I'm letting my dead husband down. Questioning if he would approve of the decisions I'm making now. Wondering if he were here, what would he say? It doesn't matter that our lives, our circumstances have changed, I still have to make the decisions alone. I just have to hope and pray I'm doing the right thing. That the decisions I make today won't screw up my child too badly tomorrow."

-Duff, C. (2019, January 8).

Hope for Widows Foundation

I had to accept that Michael was gone
I had to embrace that life moves forward
I wanted to give my all to him even though I wasn't going to feel
his embrace for years to come
Every day he pushed me to be better
He has shown me a different view on life
How precious it is to have my freedom
He encouraged me to embrace that luxury everyday

We talked about the big things—
The hard consequences for our actions
We talked about the little things
His words were uplifting
He had such a positive outlook on life
While he was confined to the prison of his mind—
He helped me escape mine

He was the excitement in my day
My shoulder to cry on
He helped me understand what to be grateful for—
To count my blessings
To take full advantage of my freedom
in the most positive way

He healed me every time I heard his voice
His support has changed me
So much joy and happiness filled my heart now–
I viewed my sadness in a different way

He showed me a level of support I didn't know existed

He reminds me of Michael in so many ways
Looks, energy, and love
I am allowing myself to open up again and
to speak freely about anything

I am encouraged to heal
It is genuine and real
This is something I have never known
He gives me strength–

On March 13, 2024, my cousin Nyeson passed away
He was driving outside of Visalia on his way to work
He went head on with a semi-truck
A fatal car accident
A fucking tragedy

One I wasn't prepared for
No one is ever prepared to be shattered again

When I got the call my heart sank
I closed my eyes–
I was immediately taken back to the crystal-clear Hawaiian
waters under the shade of palm trees

These moments we created will be
etched in my heart forever

Debris scattered across the highway
The acrid scent of burning rubber and scorched metal

The sharp tang of gasoline and smoke
A grim reminder of how lethal it can be—
The force of impact

Blaring sirens painted the backdrop of urgency
flashing lights from emergency vehicles
The whirring of helicopter rotors overhead—
Voices from first responders yelling for assistance
got him out of the car just in time

Just before flames leaped from the wreckage
Twisted metal and shattered glass
Firefighters work quickly dousing the flames
Paramedics evacuating him in a helicopter

Emergency surgery
Everything necessary to save his life

The hospital air was cold and sterile
A sense of foreboding settling in

We waited
We prayed
The surgeons worked tirelessly

He was surrounded—
A sea of blinking monitors and
the rhythmic beeping of life-support machines

The car accident had wreaked havoc on his body—
Shattered bones
Ruptured organs
A violent head trauma

Despite the meticulous care and precision of the surgical team,
the damage was unrepairable

Nyeson had suffered a stroke
He was sentenced to life support

The surgeons finally emerged
They carried with them the heavy weight of bad news

The stroke had compounded the injuries
The loss of blood flow to the brain
left little hope for recovery

Devastation consumed us
The slow realization he was never coming home
Everything was in slow motion
I felt hollow

The noise of the machine's repetitive beeping
was like a heartbeat without a pulse

The ventilator's rhythmic hiss reminding us
it was the only thing keeping his body alive

It was time to make a choice–
Heaven needed him more than we did
He wouldn't want to exist this way

Although he couldn't respond–
He could hear us
Tears ran down his cheeks as we said our goodbyes

"You will always be with us."
"Your legacy will live on."

Nyeson took his final breath on my father's birthday
My aunt's words touched every one of our souls

*"With every death there comes a birth and when there's a life to
be taken there's a life to be given.*
"Happy birthday, Uncle Loi."

As one door closes, another opens–
Inviting us to cherish the moments we have and embrace the
moments to come

In this delicate equilibrium–
We find a bittersweet harmony
A reminder that life, even in its most heart-wrenching moments
is a beautiful and enduring continuum

In the deafening quiet that followed
the hospital room felt colder

emptier
as if life had been drained from it

because it had

It was a cruel reminder of the fragility of existence and what we
were facing–
The irreparable loss

I decided in that moment that I was going to stop–
To end this pain once and for all
To find a way to live free from the clutches of addiction

I will never forgive the man who stole my purity
I will never forget the love I had with Michael
or the bond I shared with Nyeson

I am ready to find a better way and a better path

I will move forward
with faith
clarity
resilience
and grace

"This time I am tired, and I am ready to go."

But in a different way–
In the best way
To live life, the way I have always wanted to live it

A life before drugs and alcohol
A life before I was lost and angry
A life before he took

My Innocence

Silent Plea
by Riley Sterling

In the depths of night where the compulsions creep
    lies a solitary soul

        in way too deep

Helpless, hopeless, a constant fight
Darkness surrounds
This place has no light

Alone, sick, tired, and worn
In the fog at dawn
    a spirit torn

Bartering with oneself, a silent plea
            for freedom from the chains
                of dependency

Lost relationships
Friendships decayed
Loved ones hurt, trust betrayed
Regrets weigh heavy
Chains on the heart
The wreckage of choices
Guilt tears her apart

            Her mind, a combat zone
            a relentless war
                past promises made
                    left shattered on the floor
    Days blur into nights, nights blur into days

In a cycle of pain always trapped in a haze
But amidst the despair - *a shred of hope*

Courage rises
A plan to cope

Fourteen days of sobriety
  A torch in the night
    A step in the right direction
            closer to reclaiming her light

The creature within - Fierce and untamed
  Rising from the ashes, no longer Unnamed

Naked on the path reclaiming what was lost
  Defeating the Iceman
    No matter the cost

In the silence of the struggle
In the depths of her fight

      There lies a strength
      A flicker of might

For in the heart of darkness where her habits roam–

      There's a warrior within
      finding her way home

Reflection
by Margaret Belvedere

The police advised me to take a couple days off
I laughed in their faces

That wasn't an option—
Not if I wanted to keep my job anyway

Twas the night before St. Patrick's Day
The biggest day of the year
I didn't get a hall pass

I had to pour the green beer

Everyone looked like him that day
He often wore a green t-shirt

My insides were twisted—
A hat to cover my swollen forehead

After 9 hours on the clock—
my black eyes were started to emerge
I was completely in shock

I did the only thing I knew how to do
I got shitfaced and went to bed

It was so bright when my eyes fluttered open
My head was pounding

The house was oddly silent
I felt like I was out of my body
I had so much to do and so little time

I remember rolling out of bed

and going to the bathroom—
Not anticipating the dose of pain and reality
I was about to receive

I got up to wash my hands
I caught my reflection in the mirror

I stared at myself for minutes
I tried to absorb the truth

I tried to understand who was looking back at me

My face was swollen
Eyes blackened
I didn't recognize myself anymore

I gripped the bathroom counter
I cried out in agony
My chest was caving in
I couldn't understand

How did I get to this horrific place?

I worked so hard for this new life

I was supposed to be making money
I was supposed to be living my dream
I was supposed to be financially stable
I was supposed to be happy

Instead
I was broke

and broken

I looked at a reflection I didn't recognize–

A girl I didn't know

In a place I never should have been

I was shattered

Punching Bag
by Emilie Elizabeth

I ran until my lungs felt like they would give out
My feet felt like concrete
My chest was heaving

Palms sweating
Eyes blurred
I couldn't stop the tears from flowing

I didn't know where I was even going until I got there

Ugly
Unwanted
Deceived

I was stuck
staring
into nothing

She spit venom
She knew just what to say to tear me down

I grabbed the pot of boiling water off the stove and poured its
contents into the colander

"You look bloated today."

She grabbed at my stomach
I recoiled in disgust
I was already walking on eggshells with her today
I always walked on eggshells

Trying my best to avoid eye contact

Always avoiding confrontation–

But I couldn't hold it in anymore
I was just trying to boil some fucking potatoes

"Mom, could you please not touch me there."

Her laugh rang in my ears
She was always mocking me

"Stop being so sensitive."

The venom was taking hold
She wouldn't let up
The way she was looking at me
The patronizing remarks

I continued to ask her to stop
She continued to mock me
The tension was building
It was already heated enough in that kitchen

I finally turned around–
Hands in prayer position in front of my chest

"Mom, don't mock me."

I was done with her shit
I couldn't take it anymore

Her condescending voice
ripped through what was left of me

She had already taken the rest

"Oh, don't mock me, don't mock the baby."

What did I do to deserve this?

I walked away from her

"I told you to leave me alone."

She snapped
She grabbed my hair
She viciously pulling me to the floor

She pinned me down and
squeezed her hands around my neck

My mother was choking me

Everything was in slow motion
I did the only thing I knew how to do—

I fought back

The final blow
A kick to the face
Her glasses hit the floor

She withdrew
She surrendered
Her hands released from my throat

She put her glasses on and
walked to her bedroom as if nothing just happened

I was running on pure adrenaline hot on her trail

"I am NOT a punching bag! Do you understand that?"

I screamed repeatedly
My heart was aching

What did I ever do that was so wrong?
What did I do to deserve this?

She tried to slam the door–
Feverishly searching for her phone

"Leave me alone, be gone. POOF!"

I stood there in shock...
She tried to slam the door once more
This time my foot stopped it

A wave of remorse and love came over me
I had a change of heart

She was my mother

I didn't want it to be this way
I just wanted her to love me
I just wanted to be wanted

I put my hand on my chest

"I'm your daughter–
Is this how you're going to treat me?"

She kicked my foot from blocking the door
The sound of the lock sealing my fate

"You're not my daughter anymore."

Your Mess is Mine
By Anonymous

I'm not sure how to explain this feeling

It was a release
once she was gone

She was somewhere
               She was everywhere
                             I could feel her

The wind from the beach
Took my soul into the ocean

My knees buried hard in the sand
Neck tilted to the moon
Tears streamed down my face

Headphones on full blast
               I sang Vance Joy at the top of my lungs
                             I howled into the wind

I was desperate for comfort
I felt her there

The wind was hard against my back
It pulled from my chest

It felt magnetic

        She was gone

                I was suddenly

       alone

I ran to this place for months
I found comfort in the sound of the current

The waves

      The seagull's cry

            The silence always followed

I wouldn't stop trying
to find her again

She was somewhere
She was everywhere
But she was

gone

Please Help Me
by Margaret Belvedere

I walked to my car to take the call
turning my engine on for only a few seconds
long enough to roll the window down
and light another cigarette

The carport lights were buzzing like bees
I could hear my heartbeat in my ears
Black eyes bright and swollen

Her tone - intense and angry
She had no time for this
It was 1am in Florida
My sister was supposed to be on vacation

"This is your fault."
"You saw the writing on the wall."
"I'm not helping you or giving you money."
"You need to sleep on someone's couch
and think about what you have done."
"It's time to come home. Give up on your dreams."

That was the last time we spoke
for well over a year
My older sister was always my savior–
The one who knew what to do
when things got tough
My heart was broken

I was in fact

Alone in this fight

A Book
by Anonymous

I am not sure

    how much longer

        I can keep

           holding on

If what is left of us

    is worth salvaging

if we even

love each other

    anymore

              We are just coexisting–

Silence echoing

    in a room filled with

        pain and

resentment

Most of the time

    when we are together

you just fade
    into the background

                    When I try and talk to you
                        I'm ignored

You don't hear my voice–
Not even the courtesy of a response

I am invisible

If I dare disagree with you,
you simply disappear

           So why do you criticize others for that behavior?
           You're such a hypocrite
           How you treated your own brother
           when he was grieving…

How you have laughed
'At my pain'

I wonder
if you have any
feelings at all

Perhaps in your own journey of healing–
You have forgotten I am healing from wounds too

Your wounds

You have never tried with me
I have never mattered to you

I wonder what would happen if I left–
If you would even notice

Would you be happier?

174

I wish I could write a story about us

       but the pages

           would be

blank,

filled only

with your

    deafening

silence

CHOKE
by Kennedy Blum

He was beautiful–
Intoxicating to lie my eyes upon
Perfect teeth
Hazel eyes
Confidence I had never witnessed

The first few weeks of our relationship
were enthralling

We fucked like our lives depended on it
We sat in the bath for hours drinking beer
We ran through the forest barefoot in the winter
We fed racoons even though the signs said not to

We went out dancing
We went out drinking
We laughed so hard that we cried

All the dopamine was so intense
I fell in love instantaneously

I craved being the woman on his arm
It made me feel like the Queen of the castle
He was unbelievably powerful
A career military man–
A Navy Seal

He happily taught me tricks he shouldn't have–
Things you're not supposed to teach civilians
Like how to pick police handcuffs with bobby pins
Oaths to the government meant nothing to him

He took me to my first strip club in Portland

He took me shooting for the first time

When he would go away to train
He would bring a duffle bag filled with guns
to my house

He grabbed me by the face and kiss me and said
*"By the time I get back you better know how to load and unload
all of these."*

We would get hammered
and roam the streets at night looking for trouble

With firearms concealed in winter coats
we clomped around through the snowy city
only stopping to fuck in the most public places
as snowflakes gently landed on our heads

I felt bulletproof with him
Delightfully scandalous
The danger made my blood pump
in the most riveting way

Then the insults began:

*"Yeah, you're hot, but you're not that hot.
Maybe a 6. No offense."*

That night I had a nightmare–
He was a huge demon like in the movie Fantasia
Laughing with this psycho grin on his face

He grabbed me in his hand and rammed me
up and down on his colossal demon cock
I was screaming bloody murder as he raped
me with this furious evil prick

I woke up looking into his eyes
He scrunched his eyebrows and blurted out:

*"What were you dreaming about?
Was it another man?"*

As the weeks went on he became so verbally abusive I felt like
a shell of a human.

"You have an ugly pussy."
"You should get that surgery to make it look better."
"Your boobs are getting saggy."
"You could be in better shape."
"I wish your hair was longer."
"Your shoulders are too broad."

He constantly reminded me how subpar I was—
Yet he would fight any man who even looked at me

He got me pregnant and wanted me to keep it
After arguing for a week straight I convinced
him I had to get an abortion

I was sick as a street dog infested with worms
I was vomiting every single day
I was vomiting so hard that I would piss myself
I was vomiting so hard that
I broke a blood vessel in my eye

My body didn't want that baby
My body wanted it gone

My cousin held my hand while I got my abortion
He went out and partied with his friends
while I bled out at her house
Then he gave me herpes

When I confronted him he yelled at me and
said I must have been cheating

The pain of the outbreak was humiliating
and physically excruciating

I had seven open wounds on the inside of my vagina and he
insisted on fucking me anyway
He had no concern for how unbelievably uncomfortable I was

My tears meant nothing.

I laid there as soulless as a corpse
He came inside of me even though I told him
not to and he said that if I got pregnant again
that I would have to keep it
or else
I knew I had to leave him
The passionate man I fell in love with was
actually the demon from my nightmare

When I called him to end things he cackled and said, *"No one
breaks up with me."*

Luckily he was about to deploy three weeks later
I felt like it was the universe handing me a way out

He kept calling and kept calling
He would show up to my house unannounced
He acted like everything was great

He continued to hang out with my family members
He would go spend time with my grandma

My grandma loved him and got a rosary

blessed by a priest for his departure
I broke down and cried to my grandma and
begged her not to talk to him anymore

Luckily I was able to avoid him
until he was deployed

He would call me every couple of weeks and
say that when he got home we were going to
pick up where we left off

He ignored me when I told him
that wasn't going to happen
Against my better judgment–
When he came back from deployment
I went to see him

He told me that the only reason he survived was because of
the rosary my grandmother gave him
He said he would be dead if it weren't for my family

He guilt tripped me and said that he fought for this country and
he deserved the chance to speak with me in person about
everything that happened

I went to his apartment and he insisted we drink
Before I knew it–
We were reliving the best parts of our relationship Dirty dancing
in the living room to hip hop music

Laughing
Playing
Being WILD like feral animals

All of the sudden he wanted to wrestle
We got down on the floor and started fighting

That's when things got out of control—
He had some kind of PTSD flashback
and jumped on my back

He STRANGLED me until I went unconscious
When I woke up I was on my back
I was drenched in sweat
My sweatshirt was opened up
My mouth was wet
It looked like he had been performing CPR on me

I couldn't remember who he was or how I got there

But he had this look on his face like he was relieved that I woke
up
He started kissing me and unbuttoning my pants
I attempted to get up and leave
but he wouldn't let me

I was so afraid that he would kill me

Somehow my tears elicited an emotional
reaction from him—He agreed to let me go

But not without saying:
"If you tell the police about this,
I will sick the boys on you."

He had told me in the past that soldiers often go into private
mercenary work

I wasn't about to find out how real these threats were

It wasn't until he said that
that I even remembered who he was that night
I got out of the apartment and wandered

around looking for my car because I couldn't remember where I had parked it

I could barely remember what kind of car I drove

When I got into my car—
I finally remembered that he had strangled me
I remembered how hard I was screaming
as he jumped on my back and choked me out

I sat in my car and had a panic attack
for an hour straight

I was breathing so hard I was passing out and breaking out into cold sweats

For the next couple of months
I was twitching and stuttering
I think it was from brain damage

I didn't tell anyone about what happened
I feared that I would get murdered

I lived to tell my experience here
If your mind is telling you something is wrong—
Something is definitely wrong

Get out while you have the chance

You may not
get as lucky

as me

The Storage Unit
by Margaret Belvedere

In attempts to be amicable
I put all our shit in storage–
Two separate units
His friend would handle his unit
But I still had to move it all
thankfully with his help

But I was still so desperately alone
I delicately folded his clothes
sobbing and screaming in rage

This is what abuse does to you
It makes you completely delusional

Mourning the loss of us
feeling so lost on my own
so codependent
my heart was aching

Everything that mattered to me
suddenly hidden behind the sound of
that big metal door closing
I didn't think I would ever see any
of my things ever again

All I had was the clothes on my back
the closet in my trunk and two black eyes to show
for the last 2 years of my life
I was destroyed

The Professor
by Lyra Hawthorne

I knew she would be there
I could feel it
My Spidey senses were tingling
My anxiety was through the roof
I couldn't catch a buzz to save my life
I hadn't seen her face in months

We had bad blood
Real bad blood

It was a holiday and the crowd was boisterous
They were chanting and yelling
All ten thousand square feet of this place–
Celebrating

I slammed my beer but I needed something stronger
My bestie and I ordered shots and knocked them back

"Can we have one more, please!"
"Really?"
"It's been a rough week dude."

The bartender shook his head as he
poured us two gigantic shots

I lit a cigarette
I was coming out of my skin
I couldn't pretend anymore
He cheated on me
He lied
He fucking cheated on me
Revenge

Sweet fucking revenge was all that was on my mind
I couldn't wait to make him hurt the way I was hurting
I couldn't wait to catch that bitch out
I was gonna get mine

"Heeeeyyyy!"

Bodies crashed together in a drunken embrace
The table shifted and drinks spilled everywhere

I was ready to go home
I rolled my eyes and headed for the bathroom

My bestie close behind me ready to dry my tears

"I can't do this anymore. I can't go out and be normal.
I can't pretend I'm okay. I'm fucking not."

I gripped the sink as my chest was crushed in
The ache in my heart bellowed so loud all other thoughts were
silenced

"Let's do a bump and get out of here, yeah?"
"Yeah…"

Tears streamed down my cheeks

"Thanks for being my best friend smoosh, I love you."

Door locked
Bullet loaded

Sniff
Sniff
                                    I let out a guttural exhale
"Alright let's go girl."

"Everyone is going back to your house, right?"
"How's my nose?"
"You're good, me?"
"Good."

"Johnny has a key, he stopped at the liquor store.
They are already there."

She rubbed the reminisce of the blow on her gums
I followed suit

"We good?"
"We good!"

We shared a long embrace
I didn't know where I would be without my smoosh
she was my best friend

My road dog
My day one
She always had my back
I let out a big sigh
                    a quick hair flip and a mirror kiss

We were ready to rage
The bathroom door opened
We were thrusted back into the holiday celebration
We made our exit towards the front door—
With this crowd it could take awhile

I was floating on euphoria for the moment
It was a temporary state of happiness
Nothing could ruin this feeling
it was coursing through my bloodstream
For just a second I felt happy

                            That's when I saw her

She was sitting at the bar—
Girlfriends in tow

'Look straight ahead' I told myself
'Don't even make eye contact'

My heels clicked on the tile
One foot in front of the other

'Don't look don't look'
'You're almost there'

                           and then I heard them laugh

A snide remark
Jokes on me
Not today bitch

I turned sharp
My face inches from hers
Startling her

"What the fuck you say, bitch?"

Her eyes were wide
She was a deer awaiting imminent death
I wanted her to hit me
I didn't want to throw the first punch but God damn it

I wanted a fight
I poured my beer on her head
I smashed the empty beer bottle on the bar
I knew she was gonna throw a punch
My left arm already blocked it
I was bleeding
but I only sustained a cat scratch

I was laughing as I fell to the floor
Smoosh still walking towards the front door
oblivious to the mayhem happening behind her

Arms flailing
Punches throwing
Kicks kicking

'Fuck this bitch!'

The bouncer helped me up
He handed me my purse
and quickly escorted me to the door

"Get out of here, we'll see you tomorrow girl."

I was still VIP in this bitch
She was still covered in shitty Bud Light

It was a small victory—
one I dreamed of for so many nights

I hated her
I hated what she took from me
It was far from what she deserved
I may have not got mine
but I got some

We got to the car
My mind was racing
Heart pumping
Eyes dilated
Full of rage and violent energy

"FUCK!"

Smoosh was patient
We were after party bound after all

It wasn't even really her fault
It was his

He was the liar
He was the cheater
I felt so ripped apart

I couldn't go on like this
I needed a change
I needed to stop trying with him
I needed to be single
That thought was terrifying
I had no idea how to be single
It had been so long

"Hey, you got smokes? I need smokes."

She pulled off to the liquor store
I sat in the car
The smell of car exhaust and cocaine filled my nose

"Ohhh I been traveling on this road too long,
just trying to find my way back home
The old me's dead and gone dead and gone."

Timberlake on the radio to remind me of who I was
I laughed by myself in the car
The shots were starting to take hold

I took a long drag and blew the smoke out

A huge cloud distorted the window advertisements

I needed his touch
I yearned for it
I needed to forgive
I needed to let go
I needed clarity
I needed another line
I needed my smoosh to hurry the fuck up!

She came bounding out the front door
Huge smile on her face

"DUDE!"
"I got tickets to the concert Friday night!"
"NO WAY!"
"We got tickets to Keith Urban"
"AHHHHHHHHHH!" We screamed in unison

A crisp high five
Music cranked
Fresh smokes lit
Supplies secured
Let's go!

We arrived at the afterparty
The queens entered the venue
Everyone knew what he and I were going through
We had a tight crew

It was hard on everyone to watch us be in pain
The drinks poured
Fat lines laid out
The support unwavering

I wasn't expecting to see him that night

I was still reeling after pouring beer on that slut's head
Reliving the situation
Entertaining my audience

"You got that bitch good!"

Laughter rang through the house
I felt some sort of satisfaction–
But not the satisfaction I was aching for

That's when I saw him walk in the back door
Time slowed down

I hadn't laid eyes on him in weeks
I couldn't hear the music anymore
My heart was racing
I was longing for him
I was craving his touch

Things had been back and forth with us
Seeing other people
Hours on the phone crying
Professing our undying love
The ache of betrayal ripped at my core
The anger held me back from moving on
With or without him

I wanted him
I wanted his fat dick inside me
That thrust of passion to ignite the pieces
left in my heart

The pieces that were still smoldering

Our eyes locked
I could barely breathe

Butterflies filling my stomach
He was in a mood
I could tell by the way he was looking at me–
That perfect buzz
The version of him I loved the most

I mouthed *"Hey…"*
I bit my bottom lip
He nodded toward the hallway

I followed him like a good little slut

He pushed me in the bathroom
The hard click of the lock sealing my fate

I wanted it

Our bodies drew closer
The party's muffled noise faded in the background
His touch gentle yet firm
The warmth of his hand resting on my face
I leaned my cheek into his palm
I let out an audible sigh of relief
I was home

As his lips found mine
He kissed me hard
The kind of kiss that speaks of longing and regret
unspoken apologies and rekindled passion
Electricity surged through my body
The intensity grew
The muffled beat of the music guiding our rhythm
A magnetic pull
His hand traced my hip
He slipped my panties off and got on his knees

His tongue delicately dancing on my clitoris
My head falling hard on the bathroom mirror
My hand gripping his shoulders

Feeling his fresh fade on my fingertips
Running my fingers down his neck
His skin soft
His dick hard

He gripped me up
He seated my ass on the bathroom counter
He ripped my tits out of my tank top
My legs wrapped around his waist
He sucked on my tits moaning with ravenous intent

"God your so fucking hot baby. I miss you so much."

His words piercing my veil of anger
For a moment I forgot his betrayal
I opened my legs to him and lifted my skirt

I looked at him with *those eyes–*
The ones he loved
The ones that made him cum for me
I was biting my lip
"Please take me, I want you, I'm yours."

For a moment everything else disappeared
We reconnected in a way words cannot express
He thrust his hard cock into my tight little pussy
My eyes rolled in my head
His pleasure was as always intoxicating

We fucked hard
We did all our favorite things
Changing positions

Dirty talk

Our favorite role play
I was his student and he my professor

"Shh not so loud baby.
I don't want my wife to hear us."

We finished on the floor
Our bodies rocking together in perfect harmony
We executed this act of passion in
Jamie's mothers powder room

I was covered in sweat
My legs wet with our release
I was so fucking satisfied
I wasn't going to leave this house without him
I wanted to go home
He was my home

"You want to go to my house?"

He softly kissed my salty neck
"I want to get out of here and do that again."
"Well let's go then."

He left the bathroom first
That was our plan to not draw attention
But everyone knew what we were doing in there
I stared at myself in the mirror

'You know this is temporary.'
'You're dragging out your own pain stupid.'

I fixed my eyeliner
I brushed my hair

I did a quick bump from the secret stash
in Smoosh's makeup bag under the sink

I knew this was temporary
I knew in the morning things would be hard again
We would be saying goodbye again

I fought the tears and
tried to forget that this feeling
was temporary

I threw a little extra makeup on my face
I took a long deep breath

'Come on you beautiful bitch you got this'

I opened the door
Ready to get back to the party
Tonya was standing outside waiting for me

"Whatcha doing?" She asked with a smirk
"Oh, I was just taking a breather."
"Yo pussy was taking a breather, ya dirty bitch!"

We laughed hard and hugged each other tightly

"No for real though, you alright?'
"I'm good girl. I just really need a cigarette."
"I bet you do!"

She lit me a smoke and smacked my ass
"Come on girl, let's go do a shot."

We ended up on the living room dance floor

as we always did

Just the two of us like no one else was in the room
I missed this so fucking much

I wish he didn't ruin us
I wish I could look at him the same without the pain

I was just numb enough to forget for a second
I was just numb enough to enjoy the moment

I wrapped my arms around his neck
We grinded like we were still on the bathroom floor

I would live in this dream
as long as the sun was down–
But we didn't have much time
It was 4am and the clock was ticking

He took my hand
My professor
He led his student to the car
I couldn't wait to get into bed
I couldn't wait to entangle our naked bodies
I couldn't wait to sleep until noon
I couldn't wait to wake again to our fiery passion

A fire that could not be tamed
A fire that may never go out

Thirteen years of Recreational Activities
by Kennedy Blum

My bible sized stack of notes
are all dedicated to you.

Against my will
you have become my unwanted cynosure.
I've let the best ones go—
Every time your voice travels back to my mind.

Even when you weren't there, *you were.*
I am noticing more and more–

I'm a product of our decade of solitude
and love making.

We would ponder the larger meanings to life–
Always in the nude.

I quote you to my new lovers
and they believe I'm oh so clever–
One of a kind.

If they only knew it, was you *coming through me*
that they were falling for.

But I thank you for my self-awareness.
Some people go their entire lives
sleeping every waking moment.

But now...
I find myself observing everything around me—

Completely alone.

Even in the company of others—
I am more alone than before.
In spaces filled with stupid people
spouting nonsense—
We always understood without
having to say too much.

You influence my intentions
thousands of miles away.

Invisible seemingly indestructible binds

tie me tightly to your darkest side.

I want so badly to be inspired
by something other than the anguish
that exists between us.

I want to breathe out and be rid of it all.
In another dimension we are perfect.
Small arguments over dishes and money
but that's all.

The most minuscule part of my being
will always reach out for you.
I think it's only natural.

Like an addict loves their fix—

*I begin to sweat when my unsatisfiable imagination envisions
you taking me one last time.*

Nowadays I analyze our monstrosity of past mistakes. Like
movies I replay them
and every time it becomes more clear.

I put together the missing puzzle pieces.
I slowly complete our horrendous story.

I've even forbidden you
from my late-night solo releases
in hopes of curbing
my most powerful want.

Morning fog always dissipates—

When will you follow?

Taken
by Margaret Belvedere

About a month prior
some of my friends from back home came to visit
we had lunch and drinks

It was 75 degrees out
everyone in shorts and tank tops
I was wearing jeans and a long sleeve shirt
Bruises covered, fake smile in place
my normal everyday façade

He and my friend's husband made a deal
Pills exchanged, money to be owed
somehow, I missed this
I wasn't paying attention

After he went to jail
I started receiving threatening messages
He owed this drug lord in LA thousands of dollars
They knew my schedule
where I worked
where his motorcycle was parked

what time I left the house and when I got home

I was terrified

My friend's husband

paid them $1000 to leave me alone

Informing me

that there were men waiting to catch me alone

Their plan was to take me

until they got their money

I tore our house apart

I was like a fiend trying to find my next fix

$1000 dollars would get me a place to live

get me out of this hole

I was high on the possibility

I searched high and low

in every nook and cranny

Shoes

Pockets

Vents

Picture frames

Ceiling tiles
Behind the appliances
No dinero

I was completely defeated
I slid down the wall in the kitchen
I felt like someone had sucked
the air from my lungs

I cried so hard I popped blood vessels in my eyes
The small glimmer of hope was ripped away
as quickly as it came it went

My heart ached
I was so alone

at least I wasn't kidnapped

Right Off The Cliff

by Kennedy Blum

You told me to come over

Against my better judgment

I abided your call

You told me you loved me

You told me you wanted to go for a ride

So, we hopped into your

Gunmetal gray BMW and got on the highway

But then—

Your expression shifted

You looked over at me

with a resentful psychotic smile

and drove us

straight off a cliff

into a forest of trees

I was screaming

Holding onto my dog

Begging for you to stop
Told you that I didn't want to die

But you stayed silent—
With that malevolent glare piercing
through everything I am

as the car raged through the forest

into the thick

The Pull

by Riley Sterling

A relentless storm
                one that never ends
                                my body dependent

not functioning
without it

                                nausea
                            sweating
                    intense cravings
            tearing at me from the inside

brain fogged
body sluggish

                                everything is hard

small tasks
            become
monumental
            challenges
pounding head
constant fatigue

only one more fix

another

drink

Alcohol
the center of my universe

constantly on my mind

the conversation every morning

'I'm not going to drink tonight'

dictating my priorities
my daily routine

'Just a couple so I can sleep'

consuming my thoughts
planning my next drink

calculating

how to maintain

a steady buzz

without

arousing suspicion

I am exhausted
trapped in this storm
of guilt and shame

Knowing the harm I am causing myself
the harm I am causing others

my memory is hazy
cognitive function diminishing

I am powerless
to stop it

a rollercoaster
of highs
and devastating lows

Intoxicated

finally
a sense of relief

a numbness that dulls my pain

hungover

an overwhelming

    sense of

        despair and hopelessness

relationships

deteriorate

my buzz takes

precedence

        over everything

        a shadow of my former self

lonely and isolated

    consumed by a need

        that overrides all other

        emotions and desires

today I am 90 days sober

alcohol has not had the pleasure

of hijacking my life

It's a thief of my health

and my future

A vicious cycle that feels impossible to break
The struggle to regain control

insurmountable

everyday a battle against

the pull of

the

Bottle

Molly
by Margaret Belvedere

Fast Friends
Molly was a saint
One of my regulars
Offered me a place to stay
six weeks
Save money
Get on my feet
That was the plan

I was sad
So Fucking Sad

I slept for 18 hours
when I got to Molly's house
My spirit was exhausted
My soul completely lost
Disconnected from my family
Two thousand miles away from comfort

Alone in my struggle
Heartbroken
Financially in ruin

I just drank every night until the pain went away
After a few weeks
I was finally starting to come around
Finding my way in this unchartered territory
When the devil came lurking again

Big Girls Don't Cry
by Harper Reed

He was drunk...
The dangerous kind of drunk
The drunk that brings the demons out to play

I didn't want to pick him up
I was all dressed up
I had plans
but I was there

A good little girl
always loyal
loyal to the straying dog

He was screaming
forcing me to get on the freeway

No sense
No real direction
I had no idea where we were going
except we were getting farther from home

He pulled a knife from his jacket
"Take me to the state line."

He was past rage
He was looking through me

He pressed the knife to my neck
Every time my heartbeat–
I could feel my carotid artery touch his blade

My eyes shifted from left to right
I tried to figure out a plan
My foot hammered the gas pedal

Please let me get pulled over
Please God, take him to jail

I was doing 100 miles an hour and driving erratically
The music was loud

He was louder

The intensity of the speed
The threats in my ear
The blade to my neck

Tears rolled down my cheeks
I tried to stay composed but he was unraveling

He spewed past hurts
He blamed me for things I had no control over

"Slow the fuck down bitch."
"If we get pulled over, I will kill you."

I couldn't take it anymore
I was driving this fucking car
I was in control
"You want me to slow down? Do ya? Do ya?"

A psychotic smile washed over my face
I had become completely unhinged
He pushed me too far this time

I took a deep breath
I braced for impact

I hit the breaks

His face slammed into the dash
The plastic pint went flying out of his hand
Liquor splashed all over the car

The knife—
It was out of his hands and onto the floorboard

Everything went silent
My chest heaved
Liquor dripped down my face
I could see the knife shining below my feet

A quick swipe and it was out the window
The exhale I let out was audible

He was knocked out and I needed to get him home

You know those little turnarounds on the freeway
The ones you pass but never have a use for—
Well tonight I had a reason

He was still unconscious

I was shaking
I couldn't breathe

I needed to get to the bar
I needed to get to my friends,
I needed to get to safety

But I needed him out of my car first

I drove straight to his dad's house
I drug him out of my car

I squatted in my skirt and heels
I pulled the weight of his limp body

He was pure muscle and so heavy
I cursed him the whole way
I spewed obscenities
I smacked him in the mouth
I spit in his face

I hated him
He was a monster

I heaved him in a lawn chair in the backyard
I prayed he wouldn't remember how he got there
In that moment I didn't care about repercussions

The sound of my high heels clicked on the asphalt
as I retreated into the night

I raced to the bar
I sought refuge with people who loved me
But I was not about to tell anyone what happened

Instead—
I would show up fashionably late for the party
I would continue to fly under the radar
No one needed to know my business
It was mine

I parked and fixed my makeup
It was time for some shots

Wipe your tears bitch
Big girls don't cry

Hypocrite
by Anonymous

It's funny,

I knew this day would come

that this conversation would happen,

and what would start it.

I thought that I might know what to say

that I would handle it well,

but I folded like I always do.

I let you win

I always

let you win.

I let you say your peace

without the burden of mine.

Knowing even if I fight

I'll never win,

that we will continue to run in circles

never touching the same ground.

The conversation started off nice

but as expected you crossed the line,

knowing your words would anger me.

You just think so differently.

Just another way for you to get away
with how you speak to me.

The hurtful words that constantly

drip off your tongue

could never be your fault.

You must have ADD.

I challenged you,

and like always

the tower fell.

How dare I treat you the same way you treat me! Anger filling

your eyes,

God, I hoped you would have seen the irony.

You just put the blame on me,

it was always my fault.

Having the audacity to think wrong of you–

How could I?

You're perfect

Every time you *'apologized'*

was like a wound reopening.

I could have tried to explain my side

but why waste my breath,

it wouldn't matter anyway…

You say that there is no one to blame

that it was all in my head,

that I was the one

acting so irrationally.

I wonder

if you ever stop to consider the truth,

that you were the one to blame.

I wonder

if you ever get sad,

worried I've given up on you.

I wonder if you ever realized the

impact you have had on me

God forbid anyone else has feelings.

I hope one day

I have the courage to tell you how I really feel.

This time I didn't put my trust in you,

I won't make that mistake again

This time,

I wasn't disappointed.

Restraining order
by Margaret Belvedere

I arrived at the courthouse that day
so apprehensive
I didn't want to see him
to hear his voice
to feel our connection

It was going to derail me
I already knew it

They called my name
I approached the bench
and then they brought him out of the shadows

I remember standing at the podium
The judge started talking but I didn't hear a thing
as soon as I heard his voice
I blacked out

I remember nothing except the judge telling
me to sit down
I staggered and fell into a chair

I couldn't handle what was happening to me
I had a full-blown panic attack

After the trauma of the day
I really could have used a rest
but I didn't have that luxury

I had to get to work
and on time

or I would have been written up

I took the toll road to save time
money I *certainly* didn't have

I took the wrath from my manager

I took a Xanax

Her body was changing
She was obese now
She hated what she had become
Disgusted with herself
Not knowing what was happening to her
Mother never taught her

The next time she gave love a chance
It left her helpless and betrayed

She was fourteen and fell in love with a boy that
came to the Children's Farm Home

He gave her hope and a feeling of safety
Something priceless in a violent existence

When he left she cried for weeks
He would also soon forget her
It was a story she knew all too well
He got himself a girlfriend and didn't return her calls

After a few years
Serious scenarios became mundane

Kids cutting themselves
The screaming
The begging
Suicide attempt after suicide attempt
Ambulances and medical teams in and out
were a regular occurrence

Her heart was filled with anguish
The girl she once knew was dead–
Replaced by a nasty creature

She didn't care anymore her life anymore
or the life of others
Why would she?

One day something happened to Moronica

The events that occurred that day
made her feel awake and alive

She was shook from her melancholy
She wanted to change
She vowed to be a good person to the next person who was
admitted as a patient–
To her dismay this would not end as planned

The day Cole was admitted they were instant friends
They talked about what they had been through
He was only fifteen years old

During those months
the staff were terrorizing the patients

She grew resentful
She grew more reclusive and hateful once again

Cole was her friend and she loved him
but he began self-harming; *cutting*

This was normal in the Children's Farm Home and she was fed
up with the attention it brought the cutters

Attention was only for those who did wrong

She called him names
She criticized his choices
She would come to regret this

She was in the living room that night–
Firefighters and EMS rushed through the front door

"Oh lord, June is at it again."

June was a troubled patient
that was always hurting herself

Moronica crept up the stairs
She slipped through the door before it was locked
She wanted to see for herself before the rumors began

But it was not the outcome she was expecting–
There was a body on the bathroom floor

That body
was Cole

The whole facility yelled and screamed
The chaos was uncontrollable

The stretcher came down the front steps
She watched the EMS drive away with him
She told herself

"He'll be back, they always come back."

But that was the last time she would ever see him
The next morning
She overheard a meeting downstairs

Cole hung himself in the bathroom
They couldn't resuscitate him

He wasn't coming back

Until that day Moronica had not known real pain
Pain that never dissipated

She will never forget him
Sweet Cole
He was only fifteen years old

She will forever forget the hate she spewed at him
The disregard for his pain

He will forever remain in her heart
At eighteen the nightmare was legally over
Four years in this prison had come to an end

She wasn't even excited
She felt *nothing*

How was she supposed to do life?

No one taught her anything
This was uncharted territory
A road she was not ready to travel

Men took advantage of her
She couldn't relate to people her own age
She had a mental breakdown
All of a sudden she was homeless
She ended up in a mental care facility

She was forced to take medication–
If she didn't she wouldn't have a place to stay
That was her means of survival
She couldn't falter

The doctor's overdosed her–

Malpractice left her incapacitated
She wasn't capable of anything
She needed a mental break

After surviving one night on the streets
She was in shock to see people shooting up drugs

She couldn't get comfortable in her own skin
But she was comfortable in this delusion

She attempted to contact her mother
Her mother wanted nothing to do with her

She went on a road trip to hunt down an old boyfriend
She prayed for love and acceptance
He fucked her and left her on the side of the road when he was
finished

Moronica was dull to the pain
It was just another day in the life

It took years for her to get her mind together

She was in and out of shelters
Until she finally found the strength
to pull up her bootstraps

After years of therapy and hard work
Veronica was ready to take on the world

She finally moved back to California
She continued to finish college

There is hope
There is freedom
There is redemption

Hello Again
by Riley Sterling

Dear Alcohol,
After our six-week break, I felt like a brand-new woman. I decided we could have a visit since I was going on a trip. The last five days have been fun, but also made me realize that I feel insanely better without you in my life on a daily basis.

Being able to choose when I see you instead of you making that decision puts me in control. Enjoying lunches, dinners, making memories and laughing for hours with my best friends was really amazing and I loved every minute.

However, I never again want to feel the 'darkness' that you used to bring to my life. I have found that when we are together now, I don't have the urge to let you drown me, to numb the pain. Now I want to feel because feeling is exhilarating when I am not with you.

I am ok with just a little bit, I don't need to be sensationless anymore, I only want you in certain moments and those moments are my choice and my choice alone, you have no say and having that freedom feels incredible.

You used to be the one I leaned on for everything, every emotion and feeling.

If I was excited, happy, proud, upset,
sad, mad, defeated, stressed, bored, or lonely, I would reach for you.

In the last six weeks I have found other things to comfort me in those moments and I don't need you for that anymore. I am strong, I am capable, and I am not willing to give that power back to you.

I wish to keep you at arm's length, an acquaintance, because I know what you are capable of, and I have to protect myself.

I also have had a very clear view of the darkness that you bring to my friends and family and our relationships. I hope they can find a way to take a break from you too and have a chance to see you for what you are, as clearly as I do.

It is hard to watch now that I am on the other side of this, and I am in control.

I feel so free without you steering this ship, I have the helm now.

Until next time

Be well Booze
-Sterling

Better to be with The Devil I Know
by Margaret Belvedere

It was my fault
I called him
I just needed to hear his voice,
I just needed to hash out what happened
We hadn't spoken in almost 2 months–
It was eternity

I broke the five-year restraining order…
I didn't give a fuck

We cried together for hours on the phone
We were both so sorry
for everything that happened

It was like someone had infused me with feel good
I thought everything was going to be ok

Now I was in control
Everything was on my terms
I was running the show

That's when
MY truth
became
compromised

That's when
MY lies
Started

The Mission
by Anonymous

The wheels of my suitcase clicked on the tile floor.
Loud chatter filled the air and the bustle of all the people
around had my anxiety through the roof.

My palms were sweating and my heart raced.
Please God don't let him be here.

"Esta es la última llamada para abordar el vuelo 214, con
destino a Salt Lake City."

Finally, I was out of that awful place–
Unfound by him.

After eighteen long months my mission was complete.
This was supposed to be the best years of my life–
It turned out to be the opposite.

I couldn't wait to see my family, to feel my bed, to feel safe
again, and to be away from *him.*

My mother had surprised me with a new bedroom set.
It was beautifully furnished and decorated.
I took a deep breath and forced the last bits of guilt from my
chest. I was home. It was finally over.

When I entered my new space I was filled with excitement; my
mother was holding her breath awaiting my reaction.

The old wood door slowly creaked open–
My heart dropped.

Every hair stood on end.
I was sick to my stomach.

There was a package on my bed.

How did he know where I lived?

Inside the package were pictures of us together, like a paparazzi took them. I had no idea I was being photographed, I felt violated on every level possible.

My mother was immediately ashamed.
She was so disappointed in me–
Even my safe place felt uncomfortable.

I was still not free from his sinful clutches.

I was brought up in a small town with less than seven thousand people. My father was half American Indian
and my mother is Brazilian.

From as early as I can remember I was bullied.
My skin was too dark and I was too skinny.
I had a distorted image of myself.
I battled depression.

That all changed when I got a bit older.
I started to get attention when we went out in public.
My parents became fixed on my appearance.
It turned into a competition between my sister, my cousin and myself. After so many years of feeling sub-par, I was now *obsessed* with being attractive.

In my mind was the only place these fantasies lived, in my reality I was on a Mission: To serve the Church of Jesus Christ of the Latter-Day Saints. I was approved by the bishop, the state president, and the leaders in Salt Lake City to be sent to Mexico City for the next eighteen months.

I couldn't wait to learn a new language.
I couldn't wait to study scriptures.
I couldn't wait to spread God's word.

I didn't expect things to get so complicated.
We were not allowed to have social media.
Cell phones and email were only allowed once a week and only
to speak to family.

In a mission you are assigned a companion and you
are together 24/7, apart from bathroom breaks and sleeping
you were connected at the hip.

We were young and naive with no life experience.
We had no idea what to expect in a foreign country.
We were trying out best to learn a new language
Standing out from the locals made us feel vulnerable.
There were lots of cat calls and vulgar encounters.

Culture Shock was an understatement.

Every other day we walked around aimlessly until lunch. We
couldn't knock on doors like in the US.
We had to wait to be invited in. We couldn't even enter a home
unless another female was present.

Rules were strict and I respected them.
This was my mission.
I was determined to make God and my family *proud.*

He caught my eye and I caught his.
We had a lot in common and I was so excited inside.
On the outside I wore a mask of shame.

You're not allowed to do this.
Don't even think about it.

But I couldn't stop thinking about him.

He was six years older than me.
His ex-wife was abusive and took his children away.
This added another layer of complication.
I was sympathetic. I thought I could fix him.

I was not allowed to feel these feelings.
I was not allowed to have interactions with some one of the
opposite sex. I was not allowed to be attractive.
I was not allowed to do anything.

My companion was deviant.
She was completely into him but was too naive to notice he
was completely obsessed with me.

I liked him but I had to honor my faith.
Relationships were off limits. It was not an option.
I was confused but I loved the way he looked at me.

In his eyes I was not sub-par.
I was not below average.
I was not dismissed.
I was his obsession.

The high quickly faded and he began to push the boundaries I
wasn't willing to cross. He followed me into a room leading me
away from my companion and touched my body even when I
told him to stop.

He tried to get intimate
I shoved him off and stood my ground.
We were not even supposed to shake hands
with the opposite sex.

He was lost in the lust of a younger woman.

I was lost in this sea of guilt.
I was riddled with anxiety.
This was not why I was here.
I could not keep this up–
But deep down I loved the attention.

I felt torn between two worlds - The pull on my heart strings and the weight on my conscience.

I was on a mission for Jesus Christ and the Church of Latter-Day Saints, but my parents met on a Mission.

Was it really so bad?

Things were not going well overall–
My dirty John aside, I was not happy there.
The leaders were sexist. My voice wasn't heard.
My ideas were always shut down.
I wasn't fulfilling the mission I thought I would be on.
I continued to have unsettling experiences.
Everything felt difficult. I was lonely and miserable with no support and no one to turn to–
But he cared about me

Never having any experience with relationships was proving to be a disadvantage and my companion wasn't listening to my feelings.

She was encouraging disobedience.
I was appalled, this is not what I wanted.
I was here to serve and teach his divine word, and I felt immense shame for my thoughts while simultaneously trying to rectify my actions–
But it was too late.

After hearing an inspirational talk from one of our church
leaders, he bought me a wedding ring.
I knew in my gut that this was reaching a point of no return but I
couldn't help how good I felt inside to be wanted.

We were on the radar and I finally suffered the consequences.
The president sent me to a different part of the city. I felt so
much relief. My mistakes would be left behind but I was
extremely paranoid.

I felt anxious that he would come looking for me.
I tried to tell myself that wasn't going to happen–
But deep down I knew he would find me.

He had been searching the area for me, my companion
encouraging his arrival hoping we would get engaged. She was
insistent that I accept the ring and invited him to our home. She
said it was romantic.

I sought help from my superiors.
My voice was not heard.
I prayed my peers would be more receptive.
I was smacked in the face with gossip.

I was at the tail end of my mission.
I had a new companion–
Someone who finally heard my words.
She saw my frustration and supported me.
I was so ashamed that I threw his ring in the toilet.

My insides were in a battle of good and evil.
Right and wrong, lust and longing.
I didn't want this feeling anymore.
I didn't want him anymore.

I was ready to go home.

With only 24 hours to go, I was packed up and said my goodbyes. I was ready to walk away from this.

One evening an elder approached me with an unsettling smirk on his face. He placed an envelope in my hand. Defeat washed over me. I was so close to getting away, but not far enough yet.

I didn't open it.
I didn't want anyone to see my reaction–
Especially him.

I boarded the Metro and was finally alone.

> *"We're meant to be together.*
> *I want to see you when you get home.*
> *I love you. I want you to be my wife."*

I was crying to my fellow sisters on the train.
I was met with comfort and understanding.
That was something I wasn't expecting, but I was welcomed with open arms.

I was apprehensive to go into the airport.
I was so sure he would be there.

Now, as a wife and a mother–
It makes me sad to think that my fellow missionaries believe that those eighteen months should be the best of your life. While I will always give my all to God, putting those moments behind me will always be the most divine thing that I have ever experienced.

THE CLAMOURING CLOCK
by Kennedy Blum

We ripped and raged at each other
like feral beasts.

Kicking. Hair pulling.
Face spitting. Screaming.

We danced the most beautiful dance
I'd ever witnessed in my entire godforsaken life.

It was raw.
It was more real than anything else.

We mirrored psychotic patients in an asylum.

I was in love—
This is what love does
to young ladies.

You may disagree—
But this is the honest truth:
These are the things the storybooks "forget" to mention.

Perhaps it's for a very, very good reason.

He was the beginning and the very end.
He was everything.
My guiding light and the smoke after the trick is up.
A true Magician.

With bloody fists I tore him apart
until I couldn't physically
go on anymore.

I still longed for him to long for me.
There were so many years
of genuine, honest
love making.

We would sit in the shower for hours and talk about space and
time till the water finally ran cold.

Look at us now.
We'd sold our souls.

I closed my eyes and felt his
hot saliva on my wet cheeks.

A very small part of me wanted to reach out and kiss him
deeply–

But I tucked those thoughts deep within myself and head
butted him instead.

I locked it all away—
For good this time.
I swore to myself–
This time would be different.

Deception. Wastelands. War itself.
I sobbed like I had just felt Death's lick.

The poised Grim Reaper loomed over
us closely that night.

I could smell him everywhere.

I slapped myself in the face
to get a hold of my mind one last time.
I screamed to sober my emotions.

The feeling of wanting to forget someone
and wanting them to be all yours
is a troublesome situation.

I wanted to be free.
I wanted to be his little pet.
We were poisoned by the past.

Love is the clamour of a ticking clock
even after your time is up.

Love is broken fingers and smashed toes.
Love is the sound of the first bird chirp in the morning after
staring at the cracks in the ceiling
all night.

Love is knowing of the impending doom
                    and going to war anyway.

Easter Sunday Massacre
by Margaret Belvedere

The Easter holiday was approaching
Molly had no plans
I lied to her…

I said I was going to see my cousin
in Huntington Beach

Instead–
I drove to San Diego to see him

We met at a hotel
I arrived first
I sat at the hotel bar sipping a dirty martini

Finding total exhilaration in the fact that
No one knew where I was
It was my dirty little secret

I was hiding in plain sight
It felt naughty and wrong

I was salacious and lustful
I was throbbing
My panties were already wet

I couldn't wait
to fuck him

When he pulled up on his motorcycle
My heartbeat was audible
The last time I saw him was in court
over a month ago

I had a full-on panic attack and had
to be assisted off the stand
It was not my best day...

But today
I was like a sex fueled animal
The smirk on my face
My lips between my teeth
The fire in my eyes

The blindness

THE FUCKING SELF-DESTRUCTION
at an all-time high–
But I couldn't wait to touch him

His eyes met mine
The pull was magnetic
He took his helmet off and
threw his backpack on the ground

He rushed to me
picking me up swiftly

My legs wrapped tightly around him
He kissed me…

Electricity rushed through my body
I was in a love bomb fucking haze

The wounded animal in me was thriving
It was ecstasy to feel his touch after everything
that we had been through

For a weekend–
I didn't have to be alone

We barely made it through the hotel door
with our clothes on

He threw me on the bed–
I had been fantasizing about this moment
for months

That initial penetration
you know the one
the one that blows your head back

He thrust his hard dick inside me
Pure ecstasy
We fucked hard
We drank at the bar
We fucked again
We went to the pool
We went to dinner
We fucked in the car in the parking lot

We were like animals in heat
I couldn't get enough of him

He always had this persona when we went out
He turned into a different person
in the most attractive way

He was dapper
He had this 1920's old money vibe about him
I was completely under his spell

Our last day together was excruciating–
We laid in the bathtub for hours
caressing each other and crying

I didn't want to leave him–

My codependency was back in full force
I was going to find a way to make this work

After everything

I just willingly signed up
to go
back to hell

Daddy
by Aliyah Jordan

Two shots were heard just before 11pm on 06/26/23.
It is a day that will remain etched in my mind forever.

My father was gone.
He took himself out of this world
and took his wife with him.

My father was a wonderful man with the biggest heart.
He was caring, hardworking, and creative.
He loved to work with his hands.
There wasn't anything he couldn't fix or build.

But my father was in pain.
Silent scars plagued him–

The loss of his father at a young age, followed by the loss of
his mother and eventually his brother left a huge hole in his
heart. There was an enormous amount of pain and heartache
that left him full of unresolved trauma.

He searched for comfort in the bottom of a bottle–
And that bottle always ended up empty

His needs never met. His wounds never healed.
He masked his pain with another cocktail.
It left his family to suffer.

I don't think I ever lived for myself.
When I was growing up–
My focus was always to love and support him,
to make sure he was okay mentally and physically.
I had taken on the role of a parent and he the child.

My mother loved him deeply, but over time the man she once loved transformed into someone else.

She fought for twenty-five years.
Nothing was ever good enough.
Nothing was ever going to make him happy.
Nothing was going to make him put down the bottle.
Divorce was the only option.

That's when he fled to Portland in hopes of a new life.
This was the beginning of the end for him.
The next four years things went from bad to worse

He got himself a new wife.
A new toxic relationship.
A new reason to drink.
The downward spiral had begun…

I had given him my all—
Phone calls.
Endless love and support.
Encouraging words.
Nothing helped.
I lived in a state of constant worry.

They had huge fights. He was in and out of jail.
The deeper the depression, the stronger the drinks—

That's when the suicidal thoughts emerged.
It was his breaking point.
He lost everything. He was homeless and helpless.
He had a five-year restraining order filed against him.
His wife threatened to file for divorce.

He had no place to call home.
There was no hope in sight.

I continued to support him - but you can't help someone who doesn't want to be helped.

You can't make someone get sober.
You can't get inside someone else's head.
You can't take someone's pain away.

Even though I prayed every day that I could–
The events that occurred that day
ripped two families to shreds.

His wife's kids were there and called 911.
They witnessed this horrific event.

She passed away at the hospital later that evening. My father was pronounced dead at the scene.

I was in utter disbelief at his actions…
My father was not a murderer–
This was not the man I knew.

He had such a big heart.
But he let the devil take it from him.

His name in the headlines.
He was labeled a murderer and an abuser.

Day after day I relived the story through the news.
I was sick with grief.
And now tasked with planning my father's funeral.

I wanted to do right by him and have a nice service for the man I knew and loved so much.

A man that will forever be my daddy.

I was met with callous backlash.
Harsh words spewed through the GoFundMe page.

Your dad is a murderer
Like father like daughter

I didn't ask for any of this.
I was just trying to do what was best as his child.
What my father did was very tragic but I never want to look at him like a murderer.

I wish so many things could have been different.
I wish I could still hear his voice.
I try and accept what happened and let go–

But it is really hard living with this truth everyday.

To his wife's family
I pray every day that she is resting easy
and her children have my heart

I know that God
will watch over them
giving them a safe and meaningful life
until they can see her again

In loving memory of

Erica & James Jordan

Chains
by Riley Sterling

In shadows deep
Deafening silence reigns
I stand a vessel
Cracked by pain

Each shattered shard
A silent scream
Stuck in this nightmare
Lost within a dream

My voice a whisper drowned in fear
As violent murmurs are drawing near
I feel the gravity of each brutal blow
Leaving scars unseen
A soul lying low

Within these walls my spirit breaks
Identity lost
I live beneath the ache

A stranger in the mirror's gaze
With haunted eyes
Trapped in a maze

I yearn to flee to break free from chains
But in fear's cold grip
My will restrains

The world outside a distant land
As I endure each day
Beneath his cruel hand

Each day a battle
A fight to survive
Against the darkness that clouds my skies
Yet still I dream of wings to soar
To find the strength to fight once more

But know this
Though broken I may seem
Within me burns a flicker, a gleam
For hope endures
A secret light shines bright
Guiding me through my darkest night

One day I'll rise I'll take my stand
Against my tyrant's ruthless hand
No longer a victim

But a warrior bold
Breaking free
From the chains of old

Back to hell
by Margaret Belvedere

I LIED
TO EVERYONE
ABOUT EVERYTHING

Who I was spending my time with
My imaginary friends
What I was doing
Where I was going

Why I had to leave work early or come in late
I pretended to live with Tabitha
She was a real person
But we had only hung out a few times
I disgusted myself

We had an agreement
I was not giving him any money
I had my own bank account
and he was not to lay a hand on me

This was not a relationship
It was a means to survival
We both had nowhere to go
Our "couch hopping" had come to an end
We only had each other

All my savings from the last six weeks
went towards the deposit
and first and last month's rent
Our apartment was awful
The neighbors were worse
A section 8 approved complex - It was a tiny studio
The kitchen table on the balcony

blistering in the sun
He slept on the couch
I slept on a mattress on the floor in the bedroom

We did our best to get along–
But the lies continued

He was still addicted to pain pills
He was screwing the neighbor downstairs
He was stealing from me
He lost job after job and didn't have a car
He lied about everything

It was just a continuation of the pain he caused me and I
willingly walked into this nightmare

*"Sometimes you just have to give up on your dreams and come
home."*

HELL NO

I will fight to the death to get through this
I will come out on top of this
I will

That is what I always told myself
That's how I got through every shitty day
My determination and strength of will

Bug Splatter
by Harper Reed

We were kids
Young dumb and full of cum
We couldn't keep our hands off each other–
Or anyone else for that matter

We had both cheated and lied
We loved each other hard but we fought harder
We threw blows like animals

We were broken before we even began
Seven years on and off
Jail visits, parties, sex
Way too much cocaine

A threesome that turned into a relationship
His wife & his mistress
A twisted relationship born out of convenience because I didn't
want to admit that

I deserved better

I didn't want to miss the next party
I didn't want to fracture the crew's infrastructure
I stopped by for a drink and a line–*Standard*

Our dog had no food
He had been feeding him McDonald's
He admitted with a chuckle

There were Mike's Hard Pink Lemonade bottles
in the recycle bin in a house full of boys...

I certainly didn't drink that shit

Rage spewed from my lips
Words cut him deep
He shoved me into the stove—
The small of my back imprinted on the knobs hard
The dog was yelping and whining
He didn't like it when we would fight

I shoved him hard
He flew into the kitchen table
I grabbed my purse and ran

I made it to the car and got the engine started—

Where the fuck is my phone?
Jesus Christ please don't let it be in the house

I was hyperventilating
He came sliding into the driveway
The ice and snow slowed his pace
My headlights revealed the rage in his eyes
He was beating on the windows
Screaming and yelling
I threw the car in drive
He launched himself on my hood—
Hanging on for dear life
He thought that was going to stop me
It didn't
I whipped that car out of the driveway onto the main road and
floored it

I was going seventy miles an hour and screaming at the top of
my lungs with him on the hood of my car

I couldn't see a thing
I finally turned around and headed back to the house—
The bug still on the windshield

The neighbors had called the cops
They pulled in the driveway shortly after we returned

He was back to beating on my windows
Kicking and screaming
I remained sheltered in the safety of my car
He was finally in handcuffs—
Face on my hood - eyes glued to mine
The police found cocaine residue on a bag and on the cards in
his wallet

They questioned me but I played dumb
The repercussions if I opened my mouth were written all over
his face

They hauled him into the police car and allowed me to return
home

He may have escaped but our war was far from over

We would live to fight
another day

The Fight
by M. Silk

I was overlooked and dismissed
Defeated
Violated and used
Discarded
I had no other choice
I had to Fight

I had to Fight through birth
to gain life
Only to Fight off death
throughout life

I had to Fight
to keep their words from cursing me
their eyes from hating me
to keep their demons out of me

I had to Fight
to keep their hands off me
to take the beating
I had to Fight
to keep my innocence
to keep their pricks from getting inside of me

I had to Fight
to stay awake

Fight in my sleep
Fight to be safe
I had to Fight
to be heard
to be seen
to feel beautiful

I had to Fight my ugly

I had to Fight
my family
my friends
the haters

I had to Fight
as a wife
as a mother

I had to Fight
in court
in these streets

I had to Fight
in the city
in the desert

When will this Fighting end?

I had to Fight
to be strong when I felt weak

All my life I had to Fight
to keep my head up high
to keep hope and my soul alive
to find peace

I had to Fight
myself for Myself

I had to Fight
to make my life thrive

I had to Fight

to not let go
while I fought to hold on

I Fought the truth while I Fought through the lies
to endure the pain
to hold back my anger

I had to Fight
to not release my wrath

I Fight
to honor myself
to keep my temple clean
to not show my dark side

I Fight to not hide my shine
to weather the storm

I Fight
to be loved

I Fight
for attention

I Fight
through rejection
through my perfect imperfections

I Fight
through my anxiety
my depression
my struggle

I Fight
through their jealous words
to keep the peace

the joy
the confidence

I Fight to trust
the blame
the shame

I Fight to keep my senses
I Fight not to go insane
I Fight and I lose
I Fight until I win

I Fight the enemy

I Fight through
denial
sorrow
and defeat

I Fight to stay alive
I Fight not to die

I Fight BIG
I Fight small
I Fight for my faith and with my spirit
My heart
My mind
My voice

I Fight with my fists
I Fight for my people
I Fight for the weak
I Fight because they can not

I Fight for my dreams
I Fight for protection
I Fight not because I want to
but because I am forced to

I Fight because I have to
I Fight because that is all I know

I Fight my past
I Fight my present
I Fight for my future

I will FIGHT till death
I will FIGHT on

FIGHT

Hopper
by Margaret Belvedere

We decided that we needed some joy in our lives because
things were so shitty

I was resistant to the idea but he assured
me that it would be good for us
So we adopted a dog

A three-legged chihuahua named *Hopper*
We loved him because he was special
also because he had friends who
lost their legs in the war

It was meaningful to us

One day while I was at work he called me
and told me Hopper was gone
He had a seizure and suffocated on his vomit

Again
My gut said otherwise

Somehow without a car he managed
to get the dead dog to the vet
and go to a Petco to get a name tag
in remembrance of him
all before I rushed home from work

This was a new level of fucked

The flood of familiar pain washed over me
Another loss under suspicious circumstances

was once again proving to be unbearable

When I finally got to the vet to see his frozen body–

The vet pulled me aside and told me
that his story didn't add up

She said the wounds inflicted were indicative
of something aggressive

Hopper's body was covered in road rash
It looked like he had been ripped up and down
on the pavement

I saw RED
I was throwing things in the exam room
Screaming at the top of my lungs

We had a full on blow out fight in the
exam room at the vet's office

The staff were in shock; silent stares

I was too angry to be embarrassed
I was grateful that I wasn't arrested

He left on foot
I left in my car

Fuck this piece of shit

I wanted him to die

My heart was so broken

not just Snoop but now Hopper too…

I couldn't deal with this pain anymore

It had all crossed a barrier
that I didn't even know existed

I was done
Whatever the fuck this was

It was over

And that's when I met Janna

Goodbye
by Margaret Belvedere

Janna was a regular at our local watering hole
She was fun and funny, and we were fast friends
She was a nice girl from the bar that needed
help moving some furniture

Of course, being the charming snake he was
He offered our help

It was fate
We arrived at her house
It was an actual home–
In a nice neighborhood with a backyard
She had a spare room with nothing in it
except a bookshelf and some boxes

My target was set, this was my way out,
I pleaded my case in secret
in between shots and smoke breaks

She agreed
$800 a month for a room
Whenever I was ready to pull the trigger
I already had

On our way back from the supermarket one day
things got heated in the car and
he put his hand on the side of my face
and shoved it into the window

I will never forget this moment
I didn't flinch
I didn't react
I just looked at him and said

"This is over."

It was the moment I reclaimed my power
The moment I metaphorically
grabbed him by the balls

It was over—
Truly over
I was leaving and for the first time
I had a place to go

Goodbye–
The abrupt change sent him spiraling
We gave all our furniture to the family downstairs They didn't
have a bed or a fridge
We sold everything that day

I had nothing left in that house accept my
clothes and personal belongings

I was out
and he was moving back to his home state

I was finally free

I rolled up that door of my storage unit
with vengeance

I was taking my life back

My mattress
My sheets
My memories
My clothes

Oh god
My clothes
My washer and dryer
My refrigerator
My pictures and journals

My whole world came back to me
Everything was going to be ok

He was gone for good
I was finally on the upswing
After years of trying to escape his hell

Six weeks later
I got a DUI

The After Party
by Harper Reed

It was pitch black out
Two o'clock in the morning and pouring rain
I remember the smell of the wet grass
My sneakers pounded rhythmically on the asphalt

The rain was beating on rooftops and
metal mailboxes and trash can lids

I could barely breathe but I had to keep running–
He was chasing me

We had just left the club and everyone was drunk
We shouldn't have been on the road

The music was on full volume
We were all soaking wet –
laughing and yelling as we sang along to the radio

It was all chaotic
He started a fight with me in the car
All our friend's there to bear witness

No one liked this version of him
We were already six deep in that car
There wasn't much room for a physical altercation.

He smashed my face on the window
I saw stars and everything went quiet

There was a split second of silence before I snapped back to
reality

The music was blaring

Everyone was yelling at him
His laughter was echoing above it all
He grabbed me and bit my shoulder
I demanded to get out of the car
I left my belongings and started to run

He was athletic
Built like a Gladiator
I grew up in this neighborhood

That was my only advantage

I heard his steps coming closer as I lost steam
I braced for impact–

He tackled me to the ground
I had a mouth full of grass and dirt in my teeth
My nose was throbbing
I tasted blood
It was a flavor I knew all too well

He ripped me off the ground
He tossed me around like a ragdoll
He threw me over a fence and drug me across a stranger's
moonlit backyard

He was in the full throws of this weekend's bender
I was paying for my smart mouth
I refused to be silenced no matter what the cost

He was the liar–
Not me

It was blazing hot outside - stifling humidity
My jeans were soaked
My halter top was inches from exposing my breasts

I could barely breathe or move my legs—
Much less defend myself

My jeans were ripped and my knees we scraped
Raw, aching, and oozing

Suddenly he disappeared,
The rain was coming down in sheets now
I could barely see right in front of me

I was a sitting duck waiting for the next play

My eyes dilated
Fight or flight
I was ready for the next round
I wasn't done running
I saw an opportunity

I knew the house to my left
If I ran alongside their fence it would take me back to the main
road by the liquor store and a pay phone

I made my break—
I ran until I physically couldn't run anymore
I rushed into the liquor store
I begged strangers for change

I called my mom and she was on her way
I bummed a smoke and found shelter behind a building under
the awning

I hid and waited for my mother to arrive
I had a one-track mind—
Get my dogs and my shit and get out of his house
Mom was my getaway driver
She sped off into the night

We were two criminals ready for our B&E

I took the screen off and climbed through the bedroom window
as my mother boosted me in
I was in and out of there in under three minutes
The terror of his return quickened my pace
One mom, two dogs, and a few bags of clothes then
I was on my way back to safety

I was tucked in bed
The dogs at my feet and a soft pillow under my head
A day ahead to rest and sleep off this hangover
A day to reflect on the night and cut the ties for good

That's when I heard the tapping on my window
A low growl from the foot of the bed
My heart dropped and my eyes were wide
My throat instantly dry
He was here

The Unforgiven
By Anonymous

It's like clockwork once again
You want someone else to fix your problems

Once again the responsibility
is somehow not yours

I need to forgive you
I need to do the work
I need to take the time
But for what?
For you to move on
For you to let go and feel better?

What about us?
What about all the things you stole from me?
What about all the things you stole from my sister?

Her life was taken away because of your choices
Your lack of accountability
Your lack of parenting
Your lack of self esteem

All the experiences we didn't have
All the opportunities missed
They were missed because of you
Because of your selfishness

What about my dreams?
What about my career goals?
I wanted to be a part of a team
I wanted to be involved
I wanted to be popular
It was easier for you if I wasn't

It was easier for you if my dreams were crushed
It was easier for you if you didn't have
any obligations as a mother

Does it feel easy now?
Now that you're in pain and withering away
Now that you're feeling the ache of regret
A yearning to handle all this unfinished business

What more business do you have to control us?
We can't shake your daunting oppression over us
We still feel your expectations

Even though we can't hear your voice and criticisms anymore -
it lives inside us

You're too ashamed to face me
because you are riddled with such guilt

Forced to be stuck in this purgatory
Alone
The place you hate the most

Part of me doesn't feel sorry for you
Part of me thinks you deserve to live in this hell
You made us live there with you our whole lives

We lived with a fucking demon on fire

Even in your death you were ripping our lives apart
It was still more about your vanity and watching your
STUPID FUCKING SOAP OPERAS
than acknowledging the energy
 we were putting into caring for you

You lied to my sister and you lied to me

You continue to lie to yourself

You don't need me to forgive you
for you to move on

You need to come square with

Your choices
Your faults
Your guilt

You need to do the work
You need to forgive yourself
That's what your unfinished business is
No one is holding your hand this time Mom
No one is cleaning up your mess

NO ONE

Until you fix your mistakes
You will remain

unforgiven

The Gazelle
By Margaret Belvedere

It was Larry's Birthday
He was a regular at our bar
I didn't even want to go but I promised
Janna I would get a cake and a card because
she had to work late
I hurried after work to pick up the supplies
and get to the bar before him

I had five beers and three shots
The usual
I was a fully functioning alcoholic
I remember getting in my car
I was right behind Janna as she was leaving

The next thing I knew I was sitting at the light getting ready to
turn into our neighborhood

How the fuck did I get here?
Oh God, this is not good

I am almost home
Focus girl, focus

Lights out

I turned the corner onto my residential street
I passed out with my foot on the gas
BAM
BAM
BAM
I smashed into three parked cars
and flipped mine over in the process

I was upside down dangling from my seat belt
As I came to a flood of emotions hit me
This was the *LAST* thing I needed right now

I smashed the buckle hard
All one hundred and fifty pounds of me
Landed straight on my neck

I wretched in pain
Glass was everywhere
I felt someone grab me
A man pulled me from my overturned vehicle

I remember finally standing up and
looking at my spinning tires in the streetlight

What the fuck did I do?

He was talking a mile a minute
but I couldn't understand what he was saying

Holy shit am I that fucked up?

He was speaking Spanish and
I said, *"Gracias"* then took off running

I was wearing my work uniform–
A black tank top and black booty shorts
with knee-high green socks

I was leaping over driveway and dips in the sidewalk
like a god damn drunken gazelle

I flew through the front door
Janna prepared me for jail
"It's going to be cold." she said

I put on some layers–
Sweatpants and slippers
She wrote her phone number on my arm
in permanent marker

I was as ready as one could ever be to go to jail

If I wasn't so *God damn responsible*
and promptly updated my
Insurance information after my move
the cops wouldn't have even known where I lived

The police arrived
I surrendered
Cuffed and booked
Twelve-hour hold

When I was released I had no phone or purse
It was withheld as evidence for 72 hours

Hit and run
Fleeing the scene
Three Accounts of Destruction of Property

I needed a lawyer
I needed comfort
but I did exactly what I didn't need to do–
I called the Devil

His flight was booked before we hung up the phone

Resilience

You know, it's incredible how resilient we are.

We quickly forget how bad a situation, or a person once was, or how much a hangover sucks.

Once the pain has diminished, we're ready and raring to do it all over again, no matter the repercussions, because for a fleeting moment it feels worth it…

When reality hits you realize how hard it is to have a healthy relationship after a traumatic experience, or the regret washes over you after one night of drinking when you've been sober for months.

This is where we learn, this is where we grow.

Resilience is our ability to recover quickly from difficulties; it's our instinctive capacity to bounce back tougher, wiser, and more empowered.

Every challenge faced and every obstacle overcome on this journey strengthens our ability to last—

These challenges teach us about our inner strength and our potential for renewal.

The stories you have just read are reminders of this powerful resilience.

They demonstrate that while the path to recovery might be loaded with setbacks, each step forward reinforces our propensity to heal and grow.

Every story shared is a step away from the shadows of the past and towards the light of new beginnings.

As you close this book, remember the resilience that lives within you. Embrace the moments of strength and the lapses of weakness equally.

Let them guide you, teach you, and remind you that every day is a new chance to shape a life you've fought hard to reclaim.

Thank you for sharing this journey with us.

Remember, in the vast mosaic of human experience, your pieces—broken, shining, or slowly mending, hold a unique and irreplaceable place.

Here's to healing, to hope, and to the incredible resilience that each of us carries within.

WHAT WAS TAKEN FROM ME

We now present a collection of quotes from the courageous authors who have shared their harrowing stories. "What Was Taken from Me" reflects not only the pain endured but also the incredible strength and resilience that have emerged in the aftermath.

My vulnerability. My trust. My naivety. My dreams.
My whole world was shattered. I also decided that I needed to
be alone for once. I needed to find myself again. I needed to
process everything.
—Allison Halphen

I think it took away all of the
sweet memories and experiences.
—Anonymous

My heart was broken into a million pieces, my trust was
betrayed, friendship, future plans, everything I thought my life
was going to be.
—Lyra Hawthorne

My judge of character, my trust, my heart.
—Harper Reed

I feel my trust was taken from me from this experience and a
little bit of my feeling of being safe. I feel vulnerable. He took a
big chunk of love from my heart. I'm heartbroken.
—Lisa Postert

Time, lots of valuable time. Potential experiences, motivation, and safety in the world around me. —Veronica Gonzalez

I feel like he took part of my life, my freedom, my happiness, pretty much everything because he was controlling my life. He was threatening me with my kids, so I had no choice. I needed to agree with him.
—La Browne

A healthy relationship with my own mother was taken, as well as trust.
—Emilie Elizabeth

At the time…Everything was taken from me. My freedom, my health, my money, my safety, and my sanity.
—Margaret Belvedere

My life.
—Connie Ramírez

Safety, Trust, being outside without as much fear, walking alone, talking to others outside my circle of friends.
—Tanya Sprague

Having control, my happiness,
my self-worth, my mental health.
—Riley Sterling

Myself, I feel like a part of me is gone,
I have to find myself again.
—Aliyah Jordan

Trust, joy & power were taken from me. Unable to trust those
who were supposed to protect and teach me robbed me from
joy in many stages of life. Thankfully, I learned forgiveness,
believed in myself and power over the things in my control.
—M.Silk

I think it took away all of the sweet memories and experiences I
had. My mission was very difficult regardless. I had a lot of
unsettling experiences while I was there, but that was by far the
worst.
—Alina (Anonymous)

Rape: my innocence. I was a very smart girl, loved school,
cried if I didn't get homework completed,
or bad grades.
—Loi' Alexis Siliuta

My kindness and trust
and my right to say "NO" was taken from me!
—Blanca Soto

MEET THE AUTHORS BEHIND SHATTERED

We bring you powerful and unfiltered narratives from twenty remarkable women who have lived through unimaginable hardships. These stories offer a raw and compelling glimpse into the human spirit's capacity to endure and overcome.

We are honored to introduce you to the incredible authors who were open to sharing more about their personal lives and experience writing for this anthology.

Each woman has generously shared her deeply personal experiences in response to our Craigslist ad, contributing to this anthology with bravery and honesty. Here you will learn more about their backgrounds and gain insight into the unique perspectives they bring to Shattered.

Join us in celebrating these courageous voices and discover the diverse journeys that make up this powerful collection.

My name is Ally, I was born in a small town in Maryland and after earning my bachelor's degree in psychology in South Florida, I settled down in Los Angeles.

I chose to share my story in "The Craigslist Anthologies: Shattered" because I wanted to give hope to others who feel lost, and I needed to unload burdens that I had been carrying silently for far too long. My story is not uncommon. It's about a young, sheltered girl—myself—who was manipulated and trapped.

The details of what I went through are harrowing, but at its core, my story is about survival and finding my voice. I hope that by sharing it, others can see parts of themselves in my experience and find encouragement to begin their own healing. Until now, I haven't shared this part of my life elsewhere; the act of writing it down for "Shattered" gave me a lot of freedom.

For a long time, I felt I was harboring a dark secret, afraid of judgment and misunderstanding. Now, I feel as though a huge weight has been lifted off my shoulders. But if there's one thing I've learned, it's that openness can bring unexpected relief and understanding.

If you find yourself in a similar situation, I won't lecture you. Just know that though you may feel hopeless, you are not alone. You are loved, and stronger than you think. Always remind yourself, "this too shall pass.

My name is Tanya Joy Sprague and I work with Caring Transitions, where I assist the community with relocation, downsizing, and estate/auction sales in Central and Eastern San Diego, CA.

My discovery of the call for stories on Craigslist happened while I was searching for work. It felt like a sign, compelling me to share my own experiences to ensure others know they're not alone in their journeys. In *The Craigslist Anthologies: Shattered*, I share the story of a harrowing relationship filled with emotional, mental, and physical abuse. Over just 5-6 weeks, what began with love bombing and gaslighting escalated into physical harm and relentless harassment. Even after ending the relationship, the torment continued with stalking—in person and on social media—by his friends and coworkers.

This chapter of my life plunged me into fear and uncertainty, and it was a struggle to regain my sense of safety. Through sharing my story, I hope to offer comfort to readers, letting them know they are not alone. I emphasize the importance of having a strong support system and maintaining open communication with trusted individuals. Having contributed to anthologies from a young age, I also express my emotions through art and dance.

You can find my artwork on Instagram @the_feathercollective, and I share more personal aspects of my journey on @tjoyous247.

Writing for *Shattered* re-triggered many painful memories, including childhood sexual abuse, and other traumatic events. Despite the pain, I knew my story needed to be told—especially since it was the only time in my life I truly feared for my survival.

My advice for others facing similar challenges is straightforward: It is not your fault. Don't face it alone. Find a trauma therapist who resonates with you and lean on your loved ones for support.

"My multiple traumas didn't make me stronger. It was the years of therapy, programs, and people who didn't give up on me because I thought I was a burden, because I didn't want to be here anymore. It all made me resilient and gave me back a piece of myself because I had to fight for Me. That made me a Warrior, that makes me stronger." —Jazz Thorton

I'm Alexis Siliuta, and I live in Orange County, California. I felt compelled to share my story in "The Craigslist Anthologies: Shattered" to help those who may be going through similar struggles that I've faced.

My journey has been marked by addiction and the profound losses of my children's father and my close cousin Nyesontoa. In my story, I detail the intense battles that I went through, after one night changed my entire life forever, and how each day has become a step towards healing and moving forward.

My goal in sharing these experiences is to inspire others never to give up. Every day is a new day, another chance to start again. I believe every moment is precious, and it's crucial to hold on tight to your loved ones and to always stay thankful and strong. I've shared my personal experiences in rehab centers and shelters, speaking to others facing similar challenges, hoping to provide some comfort and guidance.

Writing about my life has lifted a huge weight off my chest, encouraging me even more to try my best in life.
Sharing my story has been a blessing—an opportunity to make a difference.
My narrative is deeply influenced by the deaths I've endured and the feeling of being lost that followed. To those experiencing similar heartache, my advice is simple: Pray.

I hope my story helps you see the beauty and potential that each new day holds and encourages you to use your struggles as steppingstones towards a stronger, more fulfilled life.

My name is Blanca Soto. Initially, I thought the ad on Craigslist was a joke. I know there's a lot of fraud on that site, but I never imagined that someone on the other side genuinely wanted to hear my story.

I've been through so many experiences in my life that needed to be heard, and I'm glad I took the chance because something good is finally coming out of sharing.

I've learned a hard lesson from my experiences: Not to be afraid to open my mouth and stand up for myself.

If I can learn this, so can you. But be warned, standing up for yourself comes with a high price. I stood up and endured great repercussions.

Though I often felt alone, I knew God was with me.

I haven't shared my story elsewhere; it's not easy to talk about the scars you can't see. The scars on my soul are permanent, and every time I talk about my past, my body and mind relive the trauma.

My interactions with men have been fundamentally changed. I don't trust easily and am always on guard, maintaining a distance to ensure I'm never vulnerable again. It's taught me to be forthright and unapologetic—

Sometimes, you just have to tell someone to fuck off, directly to their face without remorse, because you are allowed to stand your ground.

To anyone going through similar experiences, remember: don't try to handle it all by yourself.

You might lose friends, your job, and even yourself for a while. But new friends, new opportunities, and a new you will emerge.

Never keep silent; speaking up is tough, but you'll be proud of yourself in the end.

I'm M. Silk, I am based in California, and I describe myself as a "Maria of many things." I've always juggled various roles with ease, truly embodying the spirit of a Jill of all trades.

I was drawn to share my experiences in "The Craigslist Anthologies: Shattered" to offer hope and inspire resilience in others through my narrative of trauma and triumph.

In my contribution to the anthology, I recount my life's journey—a persistent battle on multiple fronts. My story is a testament that while conflict is inevitable, it is also conquerable. Through my experiences, I aim to show that every battle, no matter how tough, carries the seeds of victory and freedom.

This piece marks my first public sharing of my personal struggles, a significant step for me. Writing about my experiences was akin to picking at a scar—painful yet cathartic.

It serves as a reminder of my past struggles and a declaration of my determination not to revisit them.

I believe that my nature, culture, and being has the "fight" gene, empowering me to embrace life's journey as a fighter but also untied with peace in my heart. I hope to inspire others to accept and learn from their battles, finding victories hidden within their struggles.

I want readers to come away from my story with a new appreciation for their personal battles, understanding the transformative power of fighting and prevailing.

My advice is to face challenges with acceptance, gratitude for the lessons learned, and a firm belief that there is a win in every "fight, despite the outcome.

I am guided by two quotes that encapsulate my philosophy:

"Fight the good fight," 1 Timothy 6:12

And a powerful thought by Mona Soorma from Soul Food and Instant Karma:

"A fighter never gives up. Their scars are their ornaments. They may never be whole, yet they are bigger than all their battles, and beautiful, even in their brokenness."

My name is Veronica Gonzalez, I work as a security guard in San Diego, California, a job that grounds me in the reality of everyday challenges and triumphs.

Contributing my story to "The Craigslist Anthologies: Shattered" was a way for me to release the weight of my past and ensure that my experiences are permanently documented—a witness in time.

I saw this opportunity as a crucial way to not only unburden myself but also to help others gain insight into the darker corners of our society that desperately need illumination and improvement.

My story details personal battles and profound insights, drawn from experiences that I have previously shared in reviews on Google for "The Children's Farm Home" in Corvallis, Oregon. These public reflections are part of my commitment to exposing unbelievable truths and fostering change in establishments that are supposed to help and not hurt.

The advice I offer to others who face similar battles is straightforward: move on.

Do not let those moments define your entire existence. They do not deserve that power.

It's important to remember the past—this aids in therapy, in cultivating empathy, and in motivating action to prevent harm by others.

However, it's equally vital to let go and view each survival as a personal victory.

Life is a series of battles, and each day you overcome them is a win. Remember the lessons, but don't let the shadows of old wars darken the joy of your present victories.

My name is Gina Artiglio, I am a dedicated preschool teacher in Orange County, where I nurture the minds of children aged 3-4.

My story, shared in "The Craigslist Anthologies: Shattered," is one of profound loss and continued hope. Having faced the heartbreaking experience of losing multiple children during and after pregnancy, I chose to share my journey not only to heal but also to offer perspective and strength to others who might feel alone in their struggles.

In my narrative, I describe the challenges of these painful experiences and the resilience required to continue pursuing the family I always wanted.

My aim is to show that, despite significant hardships, it is possible to move forward with gratitude and strength.

My commitment to supporting others extends beyond my personal circle. I actively participate in sharing my experiences and offering support through social media groups and speaking at the Alano club.

These platforms allow me to give back and help build a local support system for those struggling with similar losses and challenges, including addiction.

I discuss how essential it is to avoid negative coping mechanisms like substance abuse and instead focus on what we do have that is worth cherishing.

Writing my story has provided a means for my voice to be heard and my experiences to be acknowledged.

It's a reminder that sharing our stories can foster connection and support among those who might otherwise suffer in silence.

For anyone navigating similar paths, I advocate for positivity and open communication. Engage with loved ones, find solace in supportive communities, and fill your life with positive influences that reinforce your strength and resolve.

Conclusion

This project took me back to a dark place, one that I never imagined I would willingly return to. When I chose this topic for my first Craigslist Anthology, I did it because I wanted to work with individuals who had been through the same experiences that I had.

However, through this journey, I have honored not only my own experiences but also those of my co-authors. The emotional toll has been significant, but I believe the act of sharing our truths is a testament to our strength and the bad ass bitches we are.

Through these narratives I hope to illuminate the many different forms of abuse and to reach those who feel isolated in their suffering, whether it is self-inflicted or the actions of another. It is crucial for society to understand that most people conceal their true feelings behind a mask, the everyday facade, with their forced smile serving as a disguise.

Looking ahead, I envision a future where I could facilitate a safe space. A place where survivors of trauma and violence could come together, free from fear and exploitation. These sanctuaries would offer the support and understanding that every survivor deserves, fostering healing and happiness without the constant worry of further harm.

I want to remind every reader that trauma and pain are experiences that many of us share, but they do not define us. Each story in this book serves as a source of inspiration, illustrating that despite the darkest of times, there is always a path to healing and a brighter future.

"This period of suffering is not permanent; it is a brutal trial, but a temporary hell. You can claw your way out and find a place of peace, but only if you have the guts to face the darkness within. That's where your true strength lies, buried deep in the shadows. To heal, you must confront it, wrestle with it, and drag yourself through the fire. Only then will you emerge, scarred but stronger, ready to reclaim your life."

-Jessica Larkin

The Craigslist Anthologies

Dive into a world of unexpected tales with *The Craigslist Anthologies*. This unique series explores the unpredictability of stories gathered from Craigslist Ads placed across the United States.

Each book centers on a different topic, bringing you stories that range from entertaining and intriguing, to shocking and bizarre. These anthologies capture the raw and authentic experiences of real people from all walks of life.

What sets *The Craigslist Anthologies* apart is its foundation in real stories from real people. By placing ads on Craigslist and curating the responses, this series captures the essence of human experience in all its messy, beautiful variety.
Each book is a testament to the incredible tales that everyday people have to share.

Every ad leads to a story and every story promises a new adventure.

Afterword

Once you have lived through hell, finding a place that feels comfortable or safe is incredibly challenging. Smiling and pretending to be okay becomes a monumental task. Living through trauma changes your perspective, your trust, your heart, and your soul.

I hope that these stories inspire you to find empathy for others. Never blame victims for their suffering or suggest that they deserved it.

Be a supportive friend, family member, or partner—
Be patient, respect boundaries, and offer grace.

"Remember, monsters are real, lurking behind familiar faces, we must remain ever watchful."

My perspective has changed tremendously throughout this process. Each one of us endures a different version of hell, and the stories in this anthology revealed atrocities that I could never have imagined. Being submerged in the pain and suffering of these diverse situations has opened my eyes to the multitude of ways that trauma can impact a person.

I've ridden an emotional rollercoaster, beginning with a sense of power and excitement, only to be plunged into pain and resurfaced trauma.

There were moments when I doubted my ability to continue, but with the support of my husband and business partner, I stepped back, took mental breaks, and practiced self-care to regain my strength and continue.

Working with some contributors proved to be more consuming of my time and energy than I had anticipated. Engulfed in their pain, I often felt overwhelmed. Knowing that once the anthology was complete, I would feel immense pride and fulfillment for all of us. This journey was undeniably challenging but seeing it through to the end was deeply rewarding.

I am not the person I was before this began.

I've relied on journaling, therapy, meditation, energy clearing, chakra opening sessions, and margaritas, spending a lot of time processing my sadness.

Bringing this anthology to completion has been a cathartic experience, and I look forward to the joy of the book's release, celebrating with all the authors who shared their stories, and closing the book on this dark chapter of my life... No pun.

Sharing chapters with my partner, close friends, and family has been incredibly affirming.

Their reactions—jaw-dropping moments, tears, and expressions of eager anticipation—have given me hope that this book will resonate with a wide audience. Their feedback influenced my thoughts, providing reassurance that others will find the content impactful.

My goal is to normalize sharing difficult experiences and encourage open conversations about our struggles. It's essential to check in with each other and recognize that it's okay not to be okay.

Tanita Ross-Cady has been my guiding light. She has given me strength every step of the way. When I didn't think I could go on and finish the book because it was becoming too hard, she gave me hope. She helped me go at my own pace, and understand my next move, all while staying out of my way and allowing me to exercise my creative freedoms. She honored the times I needed a break and put extra cacao in my smoothie when I was ready to rage.

My husband Christopher gave me the space to take on this project. Thank you for being supportive to me when I was struggling and letting me write in bed every night for months, not participating in our evening Netflix and snuggles.

Thank you to my father Lee Saunders for always supporting my endeavors, listening to my frustrations, and reminding me that I can do ANYTHING I set my mind to.

Thank you to my sister Jennifer Haring, my niece Lauren Haring, and my brother-in-law Donnie Haring, for being my biggest fans and my hype men! Blowing all the positivity up my ass when I was feeling low and giving me exciting and encouraging feedback when I sent over sneak peaks.

My best friend from my hometown Amber White for constantly checking on me and making sure I was getting through this process ok, because she knew the toll it was taking on my spirit.

My long-time friend Holly Wisdom also checked in on me, knowing I was in the thick of revisiting my trauma and trying to navigate muddy waters. You always know when I need you and it means a lot to me, Holls! #Horseye

My bestie and chosen sissy Kristen Noel, for always being my rock, even though we have had our ups and downs over the years, we always find our way back to one another. Thank you so much for giving me your full attention and understanding in everything that I bring to the table and always doing what you do best... Listening. I love you forever! Now let's get naked and eat chicken!!! Lol

My bestie Lauren Shiebler, for always loving me, supporting me, and for continuing to be my voice of reason. You are always so good at talking me off the ledge and putting things into perspective for me. Thank you for being you... Unapologetically! I love you so much my sweet ladybug.

My coworkers Chef Alex, Kristin, Maggie, Kaile, Jessica, Brandon, Nick, Yenny, Keiki, Jared, Trina, Jocelyn, Jacky, Jerome, Grace, Kenzie, and Chloe for being genuinely interested in what I have been doing to pursue my dreams and wanting me to succeed.

All my co-authors who contributed to the book: Allison Halphen, Lisa Postert, Quinn Wilde, Carly Graves, Emilie Elizabeth, Gina Artiglio, Kennedy Blum, La Browne, Veronica Gonzalez, Lyra Hawthorne, Blanca Soto, Rosetta Green, Loi' Alexis Siliuta, Riley Sterling, M. Silk, Nadiya, Tanya Sprague, Aliyah Jordan, Margaret Belvedere, Harper Reed, and those who would like to remain anonymous.

I would also like to take a moment to acknowledge the four men who put their hands on me, took my dignity, cheated on me, broke my heart, and put me through the hell that has brought me to this moment.

Thank you for being a part of making me the woman I am today, because she is a Badass!

Thank you for showing me how strong I am and teaching me my worth. What you took from me can never be replaced, but it also can never be taken again, I have learned so many lessons.

If it wasn't for the pain and suffering, I endured at your hands, and the venom of your tongues, I would not be here today, using this pain as fuel to help others who have weathered similar storms.

May you rest in peace Bub, I know we taught each other how to fight, but our friendship remained, years after the pain was over and I will always have a place in my heart for you. DMV, I used to wish you dead, but now I hope you just feel guilt, immense guilt. Guilt that you carry to your grave, for the lies and violence you bestowed upon me, and so many others.

JNH, while your impact on me was not shared in this Anthology, I hope you continue your sobriety, take the lessons learned and treat your wife better than you treated me. RSP, I hope your heart still bears the scars of a love lost to your indiscretions, you deeply regret the pain and suffering that you put me through, and you think of me often, as I think of you.

As we reach the conclusion of "Shattered," it is important to reflect on the journey we've taken through the courageous stories shared by our twenty authors. This anthology has not only provided a platform for survivors to share their experiences, but it has also illuminated the profound impact these experiences leave behind.

The theme of "Shattered" is poignantly encapsulated in its title—a reflection of the permanent mark trauma imprints on the soul. Yet, amidst this fragmentation, there is an intensity and resilience that defies destruction.

The contributors to this anthology have expressed profound gratitude for the opportunity to share their truths. For many, this has been a transformative experience, offering a sense of healing and closure. The act of storytelling has enabled them to mend relationships and find strength in their vulnerabilities.

By providing a voice to Women often silenced; this anthology has become a powerful testament to the importance of speaking out and being heard.

To you, the reader, I hope our authors have opened your eyes to what others have gone through.

Most people do not talk about the bad things that happen to them. They walk around in their daily lives pretending that everything is okay; those experiences didn't happen. It is easier to not talk about them, to put them away and pretend they don't exist. Then they go unnoticed, no one cares about them anyway...

I hope you take away a feeling of empathy and understanding for others, and if you have been through traumatic experiences, that you are not alone, and it is okay to seek help to work through your pain.

As the editor and a survivor, myself, this project was both a labor of love and a source of profound emotional challenge.

Writing, editing, and completing this book triggered and re-traumatized my own past experiences. Yet, I felt a deep responsibility to see this project through, for the sake of all the women who courageously shared their stories. The physical and emotional repercussions of trauma are lasting, but in bringing these stories to light, we take a significant step towards healing.

As we conclude this volume, we extend our heartfelt thanks to our contributors and readers.

If you find yourself in need of support, there are resources available to you.

National Domestic Violence Hotline
1-800-799-7233

Substance Abuse and Mental Health Services Administration (SAMHSA) SAMHSA Hotline 1-800-662-HELP (4357)

Crisis Text Line
Text HOME to 741741 for immediate support

About The Creator

Jessica Larkin

Originally from the Midwest, Jessica now embraces her life in California, where she enjoys reading, painting, dancing, and creating. An avid lover of the outdoors, she finds joy in gardening, kayaking, fishing, hiking, and camping—being in nature is her happy place.

As a lifelong writer, Jessica has been telling stories and writing poetry since childhood.

For *The Craigslist Anthologies: Shattered*, Jessica worked one on one with each author, transforming their raw experiences into powerful narratives.

This subject is close to Jessica's heart because of her own experiences with domestic abuse.

Through these stories, she hopes to inspire empathy and encourage open conversations about difficult experiences.

Outside of her writing career, Jessica is a Food & Beverage Director, a devoted wife, and fur mama.